HOW TO Trade THE NEW Single Stock Futures

HOW TO **Trade** THE NEW Single Stock Futures

JAKE **BERNSTEIN**

Dearborn™
Trade Publishing
A **Kaplan Professional** Company

Vice President and Publisher: Cynthia A. Zigmund
Editorial Director: Donald J. Hull
Senior Managing Editor: Jack Kiburz
Interior Design: Lucy Jenkins
Cover Design: Design Solutions
Typesetting: the dotted i

Published by Dearborn Trade Publishing
A Kaplan Professional Company

Library of Congress Cataloging-in-Publication Data

Bernstein, Jacob, 1946-
    How to trade the new single stock futures / by Jake Bernstein.
      p.   cm.
    Includes bibliographical references and index.
    ISBN 0-7931-5781-1 (6x9 hardcover)
    1. Futures.   2. Stocks. I. Title.
HG6024.3 .B474 2003
332.64'5—dc21   2002013458

Acknowledgments

I thank the following individuals and/or firms for their assistance in the production of this book:

- Marilyn Kinney, my business associate, for her assistance in gathering much-needed charts, data, and references.
- My family, Linda, Rebecca, Elliott, and Sara, for giving me the many hours I required in writing and research.
- CQG Inc. for permission to use their excellent charts and data. <www.cqg.com>
- Michael Steinberg, my literary agent, for reacquainting me with Dearborn Trade Publishing and its outstanding staff.
- Judith Richards for her assistance in editing and organization.
- Jack Kiburz, senior managing editor at Dearborn Trade, for turning my manuscript into English.
- Don Hull, editorial director at Dearborn Trade, for giving me the opportunity to work with this excellent publisher.

You can reach Mr. Bernstein by e-mail at Jake@trade-futures.com.

Contents

Introduction

For many years, the stock and futures markets have been considered separate and distinct entities. Stocks (securities) have been the backbone of capitalism and are still regarded as such today. Stocks are considered the "stuff" of which all "good investments" are fashioned. Not only has stock and bond trading been considered necessary for the survival of industry and business in a capitalist society, but it has also been regarded as the single most viable form of investing for the general public. This view has changed considerably in the light of events that developed as necessary consequences to the speculative bull market of the 1990s and early 2000s.

Although it is true that real estate investing can be considered the most profitable vehicle for making money grow, it also requires more start-up capital as well as particular skills that often take longer to learn and implement than do the skills required for success in the securities markets. Stocks can be bought and sold more quickly, and the commission structure for stocks is much more palatable than the usual commission structure for real estate investing.

Regardless of your view, the fact remains that investing or trading in stocks has long been the traditional method of choice for the vast majority of individuals. As stock investing matured, numerous products and vehicles were offered to the public and professional traders as means to various ends. Today's investor can choose between stocks, bonds, stock options, LEAPS (long-term stock options), single stock futures (SSFs), mutual funds, bonds, and numerous variations and combinations of these.

On the other hand, futures trading has had a murky reputation (at best) since its introduction in the United States in the late 1800s. The typical futures trader was seen as a fast-talking, manipulative, aggressive, mercenary speculator whose primary interest was to trade for the very short term by capitalizing on changes in weather, crop conditions, panics, and other events that affected the price of commodities. Commodities trading was separate and distinct from securities investing. Those involved in the commodities business were known as "commodity traders," not "commodity investors." This distinction, although seemingly minor to the casual observer, speaks volumes. It clearly places the individual who uses the commodities markets in the category of a speculator, whereas the individual who uses the stock market is viewed (often erroneously these days) as an investor.

The commodity trader of yesteryear (from the late 1800s through the 1930s) was indeed a different breed of "cat" than the traditional investor in securities. Commodity trading was fast and often furious. Changes in weather and crop conditions as well as unexpected events in the political sphere often caused prices to rise and fall rapidly. Volatility was and still is immense. This is in part because the margin requirement for commodities—the funds required to buy or sell a given commodity—is often less than 3 percent of the entire value of that commodity. With stocks, the average margin requirement for many years has been about 50 percent of the value of the stock or stocks being bought or sold.

For example, a $1,000 margin amount for a contract of soybean futures gives the buyer "control" over 5,000 bushels of soybeans at the prevailing price. With soybeans at $5 per bushel, $1,000 gets the buyer $25,000 of product. With stocks, it would take $12,500 to buy $25,000 worth of stock at 50 percent margin. If the price of soybean futures increases from $5 per bushel to $5.25 per bushel, the trader (speculator) will have a paper profit of $1,250, or a 125 percent return on margin. A 25-cent price movement in soybean futures is fairly typical and can occur in a period as brief as one day or less. The other side of the commodity trading coin is that the 25-cent move can just as easily be down, therefore resulting in a loss *greater than* the amount invested.

Given the margin structure of commodities, the volatility that exists in this market is understandable. Where stakes are high, emotions reign supreme. Where leverage is high, price movements are exaggerated both up and down. Before the stock market crash of 1929, margin requirements for stocks were 10 percent. Speculative trading was rampant, and the resultant volatility created huge losses as well as profits. Those who were able to capitalize on these price movements were clearly in the minority, as they are today.

As trading in commodities grew with the growing world need for raw products to run the machinery of industrialization and global expansion, new commodity vehicles were introduced. Whereas the commodity markets once consisted of grain, soybean, meat, coffee, egg, potato, cocoa, sugar, and metals markets, the early 1970s ushered in a bold new era in commodity trading.

The International Monetary Market of the Chicago Mercantile Exchange introduced trading in foreign currencies and interest rate futures. The Chicago Board of Trade, for many years the home of grain trading, initiated trading in Treasury bond futures. The commodity market, as it was known for many years, was now the "futures market." As a sign of the times, the then leading trade publication, *Stocks & Commodities Magazine*, changed its name to *Futures*, reflecting a new era of trading in these markets.

In spite of the changes and additions to the markets, futures traders were still futures traders and not futures "investors." No matter how the exchanges attempted to change the image of the futures business, the futures trader was forever destined to be a trader and not an investor. Even if an individual bought silver futures at $4 an ounce and held them 12 months, exiting at $6 per ounce, he or she was still a trader and not an investor. The reasoning was that an investor was more conservative than a futures trader.

The investor who expected higher silver prices would have bought shares in a silver mining company or a silver mutual fund. The "trader (bad) versus investor (good)" dichotomy persists, in spite of the fact that the bear market of the early 2000s and the speculative stock market bubble of 1999–2000 severely hurt many stock investors with declines of 80 percent or more. Although some stocks went bankrupt, futures trading was still seen as more speculative than stocks.

The lessons of history are often painful, though frequently ignored. Investors who were enticed by emotions, numerous brokerage firms, and many popular investment-oriented publications (including some of the most respected financial magazines) to buy worthless stocks at absurdly high prices watched their funds dwindle—in some cases to zero. As the dust of the bear market cleared, it became evident that high-ranking chief executives and stock analysts purposely misstated earnings and performance in order to inflate the price of their stocks.

Speculative bubbles are easily seen after the fact but rarely recognized in the heat of the moment. Although a number of financial writers warned of the coming decline in stocks, the public in 2000 was engulfed in a buying frenzy the likes of which had not been seen since the speculative stock market peak of the 1920s.

Given the history of futures trading as well as its high level of volatility, it comes as no surprise that futures trading was seen as a high-risk speculative venture compared with securities and, as such, unsuitable for many investors. Other significant differences exist between stocks and futures. The study and analysis of stocks were based primarily on the understanding of such fundamentals as balance sheets, earnings, debt, corporate management, market share, and the general economic outlook. Chart patterns, technical timing tools, and computerized timing methods were used as adjuncts to these traditional fundamental methods. Technical analysis was relegated to a secondary role in the evaluation of investment decisions.

Whereas the vast majority of successful stock money managers focused their analytical efforts on the use of fundamentals, futures traders, on the other hand, were considerably more oriented to the technical side of market analysis. Paradoxically, it would seem that fundamentals might be used by more traders in the traditional commodity markets, yet this was not, and is still not, the case. Futures traders realize that by the time fundamentals are generally known, they are usually factored into the prevailing price. Technical analysis tends to be the "great equalizer" between professional traders who are often privy to inside information and the individual investor who is often unaware of such information.

Since the advent of affordable computer systems, the use of technical methods in futures analysis has exploded and now accounts for a vast majority of market timing studies in the futures markets. Furthermore, the often large price swings and substantial market volatility in the futures markets have contributed to the growing use of technically based computerized trading approaches, because technical indicators are more responsive to quick changes in market trends.

■ Enter Stock Index Futures

The introduction in 1982 of stock index futures in the Standard and Poor's 500 index and the Value Line index was a major step toward the union of stocks and futures. Stock traders, who once considered futures trading risky at best or a gamble at worst, realized the benefits of using stock index futures as a hedge against a portfolio of stocks. Futures trading gained a degree of respectability after many years of suffering a somewhat tainted reputation as a purely speculative venture. Stock money managers made extensive use of the stock index futures markets as a means of smoothing out the performance of their stock portfolios by transferring risk to futures. Stock index futures trading was initiated by virtually every financial exchange throughout the world on their individual stock indices. Currently, stock index futures enjoy a preeminent position in the financial world. At the same time that trading in the traditional commodities markets has been on the decline, trading in financial futures has been on the increase.

By the late 1990s, stock index futures trading was offered by virtually all major exchanges in the world. It was possible for money managers to hedge their stock portfolios by selling futures positions against their long holdings. And speculators could participate in the markets as well.

■ Increases in Volatility

As stock markets throughout the world moved ever higher in a seemingly endless trend from humble beginnings in the early 1980s, volatility increased dramatically. When the biggest bull market in history came to an end in early 2000, intraday price swings in individual stocks as well as in the major stock indices were immense in many of the so-called momentum stocks. Some stocks rallied thousands of percentage points in only a few months. In addition, it was not uncommon for stocks to double or triple literally overnight in the initial public offering (IPO) market.

Then, as a new bear market started in 2000, the painful reality of excessive enthusiasm, overstated earnings, and decreasing profits took their toll on stock prices. Some stocks declined by 50 percent in a matter of days, and others ultimately fell by over 90 percent from their bull market peaks. As volatility in individual stocks continued to increase, futures trading suddenly seemed less speculative than stock trading or even investing. How so? Some stocks could lose 50 percent of their value following a negative statement about their earnings or business prospects. Futures markets, such as corn, soybeans, or gold, however, hadn't experienced such massive volatility despite their historically low margin requirements. Futures trading was no longer seen as the ultimate speculative venture in financial trading.

■ The Birth of Universal Stock Futures

These events and conditions opened the door to a new and promising union of stocks and futures. The introduction of stock index futures in the early 1980s was merely a sign of things to come. The start of trading in Universal Stock Futures (USFs) by the London International Financial Futures Exchange (LIFFE) in 1998 was a near-perfect marriage of two distinctly different financial vehicles. For the first time ever, stock investors and traders could take positions in futures on individual securities (as opposed to an all-inclusive stock index such as the Standard and Poor's 500 (S&P

500) or the Financial Times Stock Exchange 100 index (FTSE 100). And the prospect of doing so on margin as low as 20 percent sweetened the dowry for USFs.

Although the cost of buying 100 shares of IBM at 50 percent margin might be $5,000 (with IBM at $100/share), the ability to "own" 100 shares of IBM in a futures contract for a margin of $1,000 or even less has opened a world of vast new possibilities to stock and futures traders. Some market experts feared that the ability to trade futures on stocks would reduce investors' incentive to own stocks. Others, however, correctly reasoned that ultimately the increase in market participants would add liquidity, volume, and numerous new strategies to the markets, thereby enhancing the risk-transfer process and with it the overall functioning of financial processes. This has in fact been the case, particularly in the securities futures markets for Italian and Spanish stocks, where trading volume has been very large.

The Nasdaq exchange in New York and the LIFFE exchange in London formed a joint venture known as the NQLX, to trade Single Stock Futures (SSFs). The primary SSF market is based in Chicago at the OneChicago Exchange. The following SSFs were listed for trading on the NQLX market:

GICS Group
Advanced Micro Devices
American International Group
Amgen Inc.
AOL Time Warner
Applied Materials
AT&T Corp.
Bank of America Corp.
Bristol-Myers Squibb
Brocade Communications System
ChevronTexaco
Cisco Systems Inc.
Citigroup Inc.
Coca-Cola Co.
Dell Computer Corp.

eBay
EMC Corp./Massachusetts
Exxon Mobil Corp.
Ford Motor Co.
General Electric
General Motors (GM)
Home Depot
Honeywell International Inc.
IBM
Intel Corp.
Johnson & Johnson
JP Morgan Chase & Co.
Juniper Networks Inc.
Merck & Co.
Merrill Lynch & Co. Inc.
Micron Technology Inc.
Microsoft Corp.
Morgan Stanley Dean Witter & Co.
Oracle Corp.
PepsiCo Inc.
Pfizer Inc.
Procter & Gamble (PG)
Qualcomm Inc.
SBC Communications Inc.
Siebel Systems Inc.
Sun Microsystems Inc.
Texas Instruments Inc.
Veritas Software Corp.
Verizon Communications Inc.
Wal-Mart Stores Inc.
Walt Disney Co.

■ Imminent Action

In December 2000, the Commodity Futures Modernization Act (CFMA) of 2000 became law in the United States. It was the intent of this law to overhaul the somewhat archaic and draconian rules that for so many years prevented futures trading on individual stocks in the United States. The regulatory bodies that would, under the CFMA, oversee trading in securities futures, known as single stock futures (SSFs) in the United States, were the National Futures Exchange, the Commodity Futures Trading Commission, and the Securities and Exchange Commission. Furthermore, steps had to be taken to avoid the creation of conflicting regulations on members of the National Association of Securities Dealers (NASD). The National Futures Association, in its various online postings, was optimistic about the "new era for the futures industry." But the sad reality was that seeds of a bureaucratic nightmare were slowly sprouting: delay after delay plagued the new SSF market.

Even though USFs had been trading at the LIFFE since 1998 in a slowly, but steadily, growing market, the U.S. exchanges, bogged down by bureaucratic inefficiency, dragged their feet, delaying the start of trading in these vehicles in the United States. Eventually, however, the new market was ready to trade. At first, only professional traders were legally permitted to participate in a field limited to 30 stocks, but eventually the market was opened to the trading public.

Although SSFs offer great profit potential, it is reasonable to ask whether investors and traders are able to make effective use of SSFs. Here are other questions and issues about the use and understanding of SSFs:

- Do investors understand the SSF market?
- Do stock investors and traders know how to trade futures?
- Do futures traders understand how to trade stocks?
- Are stock traders prepared for the volatility of futures?
- Are futures traders prepared for the fundamentals that often affect stocks?
- Are stock traders sufficiently educated and skilled in technical analysis?

Although the introduction of SSFs and USFs offers vast new areas of potential profit, there are also risks, educational challenges, procedural issues, and financial management concerns that can be resolved only through experience and education. This book provides answers to help you understand and profit from the single stock futures (SSF) market. As time passes and experience with the markets grows, so will our fund of knowledge. New strategies beyond those to be discussed here will be developed in time, perhaps leading to a revision of this book.

■ Goals and Objectives

The goals and objectives of this book are to achieve the following:

- Educate stock traders, investors, and speculators in the essential aspects of futures trading in order to provide for a smooth transition into SSF trading.
- Educate futures traders and speculators in the essential aspects of stock trading as well as provide for a smooth transition into SSF trading.
- Compare and contrast the similarities and differences between stock trading, investing, futures trading, and SSF trading.
- Explain the functioning and trading mechanics of the SSF market.
- Present specific trading strategies, systems, and methods that can be used in the SSF market.
- Provide specific examples and illustrations of trades from inception to conclusion to illustrate several trading scenarios and strategies.
- Illustrate trading strategies that combine SSFs and their underlying securities.
- Explain and discuss spreading opportunities using SSFs.
- Examine such pragmatic considerations as order entry and online SSF trading.
- Illustrate several viable day trading methods in SSFs.

Given that the SSF market is still in its infancy as this book is being written, changes will inevitably occur over time. Some of these changes will be significant: New applications will be discovered; new strategies will be developed; and new trading methodologies will emerge. In addition, there will be more to learn. Those, however, who are prepared with a basic and functional understanding of how the SSF market works will have a solid base on which to add new information. A firm footing is essential to a profitable future.

Now that I have provided you with a brief introduction to the metamorphosis and history of SSF trading and its precursors, I will address some of these issues in greater detail in the chapters that follow. First, however, a few important preliminary issues.

▌ Who Am I and What Qualifies Me to Write This Book?

My experience in the stock and futures markets spans three decades. My first trade in stocks was made in the summer of 1968 in Wright-Hargreaves, a small Canadian gold mining stock. From there I "graduated" into the futures markets (which in those days was called the commodities market). I began trading shell egg futures in the summer of 1968 under the guidance and direction of a Chicago broker.

At that time, I was pursuing my education and work in the mental health field. Because I had not been educated in either finance or economics, I had no idea that my eventual profession would be the field of trading and investing.

As the years passed, I developed numerous trading strategies and analytical methods in futures and in stocks. In 1982 I wrote my first book, *The Investor's Quotient* (Wiley and Sons). Since then I have authored over 35 books on the stock and futures markets, several of which have been translated into foreign languages. My articles have been published in a variety of trade publications.

I have appeared on numerous television and radio shows in the United States and Canada, including the original *Wall Street Week with Louis Rukeyser*. I have been a speaker at numerous trading and investing seminars throughout the world and have held over 500 of my own educational trading seminars.

I maintain two investment and trading Web sites—trade-futures .com and 2chimps.com—and several more market-related Web sites are now under development. I publish a number of investment newsletters that are read by active traders and investors all over the world. In addition, I have developed numerous innovative analytical tools for trading and market analysis with a focus on timing, trends, seasonality, and market patterns.

■ Why Trade Futures?

One of the first "housekeeping" items that must be addressed is the question, why trade futures? Although I answer this question in considerable detail later, a brief comment seems indicated now. The several reasons, in general, for trading the futures markets are these (but not necessarily in order of preference):

- To accumulate profits for short-term and long-term trends
- To protect your business or investments from adverse price moves
- To take advantage of inflationary and disinflationary economic trends
- To hedge stock portfolios by using stock index futures

This preliminary overview is intended for those who have never traded futures. For those who have never traded stocks, some of the reasons for doing so may be obvious. Nonetheless, I provide a brief overview of those reasons now, to be followed by more detailed reasons later on.

■ Why Invest in Stocks?

Stock investing has long been the favored approach to making profits in the financial markets. The basic reasons for trading and/or investing in stocks have traditionally been these:

- To participate in long-term moves consistent with economic growth
- To generate long-term profits in pension and retirement accounts
- To capitalize on short-term market swings
- To protect savings from the negative effects of inflation and disinflation
- To participate in new growth industries and technology without the need to actually be involved in these businesses

The other reasons for trading and investing in stocks are examined in detail later on.

As you can see, the reasons for participating in stocks and futures are not too dissimilar. The differences between these two vehicles are, however, significant, particularly in relation to a time frame—that is, the length of time a position is held—and margin requirements. The SSF market attempts to marry these two vehicles into one instrument that seeks to maximize the benefits of each in a grand and long overdue union. Although the idea of trading futures on individual stocks has been with us for many years, the regulatory climate did not permit such trading in the United States until the implementation of the Commodity Futures Modernization Act (CFMA). SSF trading in U.S. markets was prompted by the introduction of Universal Stock Futures at the LIFFE exchange in London. Now that the market is available, it behooves all serious investors and traders to become educated in the vehicle that promises to forever change the investment landscape. Let us now begin our journey into the SSF market.

CHAPTER ONE

The Biggest Bull Market in History Comes to an End

To understand the forces that shaped the development of SSFs, it is best to have an overview of U.S. stock market history from the early 1920s to the present day. The history of stock market trends in the United States is at one and the same time a colorful one as well as a volatile one. The market, as measured by the Dow Jones Industrial Average (DJIA), rallied from its January 1921 low of 63.9 to its January 1929 high of 386.1, fostering a massive speculative bubble that ended in the crash of 1929. Although a number of cogent reasons were advanced as causes of the crash, one of the most significant was that stock speculators were permitted to trade stocks on 10 percent margin. In other words, they could buy $1,000 worth of stock for only $100, which understandably fueled the fires of excessive speculation. The resultant speculative bubble led to a collapse of stocks that ultimately brought a low in the 40.5 area in January of 1932. Stocks then languished during the Great Depression.

By the early 1950s, stocks began a trend up as the United States lifted itself out of depression, and investors regained confidence in the economy. Stocks continued to rally until the early 1970s, making a low in 1972 from which a lengthy rally developed until the July

1987 top in the 2,740 area. Stocks had come a long way. Speculative activity increased substantially, leading to the "crash of 1987." But the market wouldn't rest on its laurels too long following the 1987 decline. By January of 1988, volatility in stocks had increased again. The biggest bull market in history was well under way.

From the 1987 low of approximately 1,706, stocks moved higher to reach an all-time high in January 2000 at the "unbelievable" 11,750 level. The bull market had exceeded even the most optimistic forecasts of respected market prognosticators. But every silver lining has its dark cloud: the bull market was not without its problems. "Irrational exuberance," as it was called by Federal Reserve Chairman Alan Greenspan, fueled stocks ever higher from mid-1998 through the 2000 top. Worthless stocks surged. Initial public offerings (IPOs) often increased in value by over 100 percent the same day they were issued. Investors clamored for new technology stocks that would satisfy their speculative hunger. In efforts to calm the speculative fires, the Federal Open Market Committee (FOMC) boosted interest rates by ½ percent in May 2000. Stocks shrugged off the bold action, continuing their speculative bubble.

Finally, the money game reached its peak. Stocks began to decline. Shares that had risen on mere air—buoyed by promoters, touted by brokerage houses, and bought on the expectation of earnings five years into the future—lost their divinelike status. Shares of companies that were either worthless or less than worthless (i.e., showing large deficits) declined from their absurd prices of over $100 per share to lows in the $2 to $5 per share range or, in some cases, the companies entirely folded their operations by the summer of 2002. The bull market was finally over. Some degree of rational behavior had returned on the heels of sobering reality. Some of the largest corporations in America had fallen to their lowest share prices in decades. United Airlines, once a "high-flying" stock, was on the verge of bankruptcy in September 2002. Massive fraud brought down the once giant Enron. WorldCom shares declined to pennies per share on revelations of fraudulent bookkeeping. Some of the most respected brokerage firms and corporate executives in the United States were implicated and/or indicted for violations of existing securities laws.

During the bull market of the 1990s and 2000s, speculative activity was rampant. Day trading was the "game" of the times. Traders who barely understood how markets functioned were attracted to the game by the promise of quick profits and easy money. There were shades of the 1920s speculative frenzy, but most investors ignored the warnings. Sadly, the new generation of traders was blinded by the promise of profits and failed to heed the lessons of history. Many paid dearly for their greed and ignorance. But from the seeds of despair, more lessons were learned and the SSF market emerged as the possible "deus ex machina."

■ How and Why Volatility in Stocks Grew from 1982 through 2000

Volatility is as much a function of price as it is a function of trader expectations, trader emotion, and trading activity. These factors, along with new trading technology and low commissions, created a backdrop of increasing market volatility from 1982 through 2000. As world stock markets continued to move higher, these factors and forces combined in a unique way to foster the growth of highly speculative activity. As long as the game continued, things were good and the future looked rosy. Trading activity was brisk, and brokerage houses enjoyed a period of considerable growth.

The shares of brokerage house Merrill Lynch were at $2 per share (split adjusted) in 1990. By January 2001, the stock made an all-time high of $80 per share. After the trading public got "burned" by crashing technology stocks, shares of Merrill Lynch had fallen to a low of $33 per share. Other brokerage firms also suffered in the declining market environment, as their credibility was injured by losing stock picks and various scandals involving preferential treatment of large clients.

At the same time, the declining futures markets, combined with deeply discounted commissions, resulted in a consolidation of futures brokerage firms. In part, online trading helped exacerbate the decreasing commission structure of stock and futures brokerage firms. In short, both industries were suffering severely by 2002. SSFs were introduced, in part, to rescue a failing brokerage industry. I see the SSF market as the intended savior—the solution contrived to end the seemingly insoluble challenges that afflicted the investment business.

■ Heroes and Villains

The scorecard of heroes and villains in the stock market of the late 1990s and early 2000s reads like a who's who of technology and high-profile executives. Stocks such as Brocade Communications ran up from a low of $4.12 in 1999 to a high of over $133 in October 2000, only to decline to the $12.63 level by October 2001. The price rise took 17 volatile months to achieve. The ride down initially took only 6!

Internet wunderkind Inktomi (INKT) surged from a low in 1998 of about $7.68 to an irrational high of over $241 in March 2000. In June 2002, INKT was trading at $1.48 a share. Clearly, many investors who bought INKT near the top and held it were burned.

But these are only two of many examples. Yes, a few notable stocks such as Krispy Kreme Doughnuts (KKD) survived the debacle. KKD rose from an initial offering price of about $7.50 a share to a high of over $46 in December 2001 without crashing. Interestingly enough, KKD offered substance (even though the doughnuts were fluffy) rather than technology. Technology was shunned because it was technology that had hurt the many investors who believed the media hype campaign that accompanied the top of the biggest bull market in history.

■ Fleecing of the Small Investor

As is often the case when stocks surge and then crash, it's the small investor who gets fleeced. At the same time that professional traders, sensing the inevitable top, fueled the bullish fires with positive statements, many insiders surreptitiously sold their holdings in a classical distribution pattern. Their task of unloading worthless stock on an unsuspecting public was facilitated by positive statements and buy recommendations from analysts who had a vested interest in promoting these shares. Investors who had missed the big moves, anxious not to let it happen again, finally gave in to their emotions, buying puffed up stocks at or near their all-time highs. Finally, when the stocks that "could do no harm" crashed, small investors were purged from the market.

Taking their place were new and hopeful investors, inspired by low commissions, highly optimistic forecasts, and the belief that online trading would lead to success. And the newcomers were ultimately burned by the bear market as well, because their orientation was bull-ish, as is the orientation of most novice investors. They fought the trend all the way down by failing to follow the path of least resistance.

The bear market continued. Brokerage houses suffered as well. Even one of the most sophisticated investment banking firms—JP Morgan Chase—saw its shares drop sharply from a high of over $67 in January 2000 to a low of $26.70 in January 2002. Without a doubt, the brokerage industry was in need of a shot in the arm. A declining market, damaged credibility, waning investor confidence, and a stagnant economy all combined to create the dire need for a new stimulus. Could that stimulus be single stock futures?

■ How the Experts Erred

Apparently, the popular thinking was that SSFs could save the brokerage business (and perhaps even the markets). But procrastina-tion, territorialism, and bureaucratic foot-dragging continued to delay the introduction of SSFs in the United States, and the broker-age community was dealt yet another blow. Adding to an already bad situation was the revelation that many of America's top brokerage firms knowingly continued to recommend worthless stocks to their clients in order to keep the commission dollars flowing.

Experts who appeared regularly on business television programs, such as CNBC, touted stocks that continued to decline, even though these experts were aware of the problems attendant on the stocks. Ultimately, an agreement was made with the New York at-torney general whereby a large fine was paid by Merrill Lynch in compensation for the wrongs that had been committed. But, of course, investors didn't get *their* money back; instead, it went to the government. By late 2002, SEC investigations were rampant as investors and the government sought victims to be held accountable for losses so many investors suffered. Even the once highly respected Martha Stewart was implicated in a stock scandal.

■ Death of the New Economy

At the peak of the 1990–2000 bull market, the so-called new economy was touted as both invincible and eternal. Stocks that represented the old economy were uninviting, unexciting, and rarely recommended. While traders and investors were being advised to buy worthless stocks like Broadvision (BVSN) at $90 a share, they were advised to forget about old economy stocks that had no sex appeal, such as H. J. Heinz (HNZ) that was trading in the $43 per share range and actually paid a dividend. In addition, stocks like Philip Morris Companies (MO) (trading at $32 a share) also offered little promise for the future. The chart in Figure 1.1 shows how BVSN enjoyed a spectacular ride up and how it has crashed since the stock market top in 2000. Yet several years later, BVSN traded below $1 a share and MO had risen to $56 and HNZ maintained its price in the $41 a share range. Investors sadly accepted the fact that the new economy was moribund while the old economy was alive and "kicking." What to do?

■ Solutions and Salvation

Marketing and repackaging are the lifeblood of capitalist economies. We have become experts at reinventing the same products repeatedly and selling them as new. We have become proficient at planned obsolescence. For many years the securities industry provided a vital service to investors by serving as the intermediary between buyers and sellers of securities; and commissions were paid to brokers as part of the agreement. As the brokerage industry became more competitive and the cost of clearing trades decreased as a result of electronic order executions, commissions declined, forcing

■ FIGURE 1.1 The Broadvision Debacle

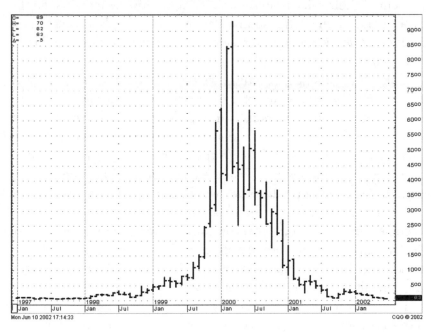

brokers to seek new avenues of income aside from the monies earned on "float" income (i.e., income derived on short-term interest from free reserves in customer accounts).

The futures industry suffered a similar malaise in the late 1990s and early 2000s. Specifically, commissions were more competitive and interest rates were low, thereby lowering float income. Electronic trading lowered costs but also lowered commissions. Clearly, what was needed in both the futures and the securities industries was a new vehicle, a new instrument, a new game that traders and investors could play. The time was optimal for the introduction of SSFs.

■ How Futures Survived While Stocks Crashed

Another positive aspect of the new SSF market was the relative stability of the futures markets, even though stocks declined sharply from their year 2000 highs. Stocks such as BVSN lost more than 90 percent of their value from their 2000 highs; futures markets, on the other hand, didn't suffer similar declines. *In fact, the declines in futures on a price percentage basis were tame compared with the declines in many stocks.*

The old argument that futures were riskier than stocks no longer held water. Several years of extreme volatility devastated many stocks, but the futures markets, although lower as well in many cases, maintained their strength without the same severe declines that afflicted speculative stocks. Perhaps the main reason for the comparative strength in futures prices was the fact that these markets actually represented something. In other words, corn futures are a tangible item. Stocks, on the other hand, are pieces of paper that can easily become worthless. Corn, soybeans, and other commodities cannot declare bankruptcy as corporations can. There is a logical, and often reasonable, limit to commodity prices' downside risk, particularly in the agricultural, metal, and tropical futures markets.

Furthermore, some commodity markets—gold, for example—moved higher as stocks moved lower. While stocks declined in 2001 and 2002, gold prices rallied from about $255 in early 2001 to a high of about $329 in mid-2002. Gold rallied as stocks dropped, fulfilling its traditional role as a hedge against economic uncertainty.

∎ The Logical Step

Although some may argue that the introduction of SSFs was the next logical step in market growth, the odds are that it was a necessary step as well. The introduction of SSFs promised to bring much-needed nourishment into the securities and futures industries. Stock investors and traders who had previously been unwilling to use the futures markets or were unfamiliar with them now had a new and legitimate vehicle by which to either hedge their stock transactions or speculate on stocks with less up-front capital.

Futures traders, who have long felt that stocks require too much margin or are not sufficiently volatile, now had a new trading vehicle that allowed them to capitalize on stock swings without the need to post the 50 percent (or more) margin required of stocks.

Given that the SSF market is a fully electronic exchange, price executions are fair, efficiency is high, and order fills occur instantaneously (provided there is sufficient liquidity and activity). In all, the SSF market has ushered in a new era in trading for stock and futures trading. The Commodities Future Modernization Act (CFMA) will have fulfilled its purpose in modernizing the markets and, as a beneficial consequence, saving a distressed industry, so long as the new vehicle continues to gain popularity and trading volume.

CHAPTER TWO

The History of Futures Trading: An Overview

■ The Evolution of Futures Trading

Trading in futures had its origin in the development and growth of grain trade in the United States in the mid-1800s. Before the existence of U.S. futures markets (originally known as commodity markets), the Japanese futures exchange in silk and rice, as well as the English market in iron warrants, continued for many years and, to a given extent, functioned as models for U.S. markets.

Futures trading in the United States evolved as a natural outgrowth of the need to protect producers and end users against volatile price moves in cash grains. Chicago assumed a leading role as the center of grain futures trading. Because the midwestern United States is the heart of a major agricultural producing region and Chicago is strategically located on the Great Lakes as a shipping hub, it was a natural site for trading in the cash and futures grain markets. Livestock trading also developed as large meat-packing houses made their home in the Chicago stockyards area.

The Chicago Board of Trade was organized in 1848, but it was not until about 1859 that trading actually started. As noted previously, the need to control risk by producers and end users was the primary motivation for the creation of this exchange. As you will see in the chapters that follow, the impetus for the creation of a SSF market was essentially similar to the impetus for the creation of futures trading in Chicago so many years ago; it was intended to fulfill an economic purpose.

The Chicago Board of Trade, once created, allowed producers (farmers), grain processing firms, and exporters to manage their risk and exposure to unknown elements, such as weather, political events, and economic uncertainties by hedging. The practice of hedging, which forms the substructure of all futures markets, became widely accepted as a viable approach to protect profits and minimize losses.

■ Worldwide Expansion of the Futures Markets

Although the futures markets had their origin in Japan, it took many years for futures trading to be accepted in all major world financial centers. Not until the early 1980s did futures trading become viable throughout the world. Even in 2002, we see significant differences in the way futures are traded throughout the world. (These are discussed in my book *Trading the International Futures Markets* (New York Institute of Finance, 2000).) Although virtually every major financial center in the capitalist world has had viable and functional stock exchanges, futures trading in all major world centers is relatively new. However, given the fact that futures trading has indeed become a reality worldwide, the door is open for SSF trading as well.

■ Defining the Hedge

The concept of hedging is based on the assumption that the movement of trends in cash and futures prices runs parallel to each other. The goal of hedgers is to lock in a fixed future price in order to eliminate their risk of exposure to interim price fluctuations. A hedger can be a buyer or a seller of futures, depending on need and current position in the cash market. The cash market in traditional futures trading is different from the cash market for SSFs. Whereas grains, meats and metals are the markets that hedgers hedge against in traditional futures, in SSFs the underlying "cash" market is the actual stock the SSF represents. Therefore, a hedger in SSFs might own 100 shares of IBM against which he sells an SSF in IBM.

The best way to understand hedging and the futures market is by a specific example. Because I'll assume that you have no understanding of the futures market as yet, I'll first use an example from the grain markets. Suppose you are a corn farmer. Your crop has been planted. All seems well, but the summer becomes unexpectedly hot and dry. Rain is scarce in most parts of the country, and the corn crops in most areas are deteriorating rapidly. Some of the large grain-processing firms become concerned about corn prices several months in the future as the heat and drought damage take their toll on crops. In your area, however, weather is not so bad, moisture has been sufficient, and your crop is still in relatively good condition. You are concerned about what may happen, but you are also pleased to see prices rising rapidly as concerns about the corn crop continue to prompt buying by traders, large grain-processing companies, and speculators.

Grain-processing companies, such as large baking companies, animal feed manufacturers, food processors, and vegetable oil producers, begin to buy corn from the farmers and grain firms who have stored it from previous years when prices were too low to warrant selling. Buying by the large companies is considerable because of their immense need for corn over the next few months. The simple fact is they need the product and will buy it at virtually any price as long as they can pass on the increased cost to consumers. Speculators who may feel that prices will rise add fuel to the fire by also buying futures. Note, however, that there are also sellers who disagree with the forecasts, but their selling is outpaced by the buying.

The law of supply and demand tells us that the price of corn will rise as the supply falls as long as demand remains the same or increases. Clearly, in this case the supply is decreasing as demand remains the same or increases. The result is a rising price trend that is likely to continue until or unless the fundamental situation changes.

Prices continue to rise dramatically in the *cash market*—that is, the immediate or day-to-day market for actual corn as opposed to corn futures. Another term for the cash market is the *spot market*, which refers to transactions made on the spot for immediate delivery, not for delivery at some time in the future.

Assume that you know how much it costs you to grow your corn. The cost of all the inputs—fertilizer, fuel, land, labor, rents, interest rates, insecticides, vehicle operation, insurance, and additional costs—have all been factored into your bottom line. Your cost of production is $1.85 for each bushel of corn. Knowing your cost and knowing the current market price, you call the local grain terminal where cash corn is bought and sold; and there you discover that the current price for corn is even more attractive than you had originally thought. Corn is selling at $3.25 per bushel on the futures market. Two weeks ago, corn was selling at $3.00 per bushel and three months ago at $2.75. You've planted enough corn to yield 50,000 bushels this year. Clearly, the difference between the market price several months ago and the current price is substantial, running into thousands of dollars and perhaps being the deciding factor in your overall profitable operations this year.

What are your choices? Is there a way that you can lock in your profit now? You're concerned that by the time your crop has been harvested, prices may be back down again and what looks like a good price now may be gone in a few weeks. Various forces and factors could cause prices to decline from their current lofty levels.

The U.S. Department of Agriculture, for example, could release grain from its reserves to increase supplies and drive prices down. Foreign production could be larger than expected, making null and void the decline in the anticipated U.S. crop size. Weather conditions could improve substantially, lessening the impact on crops. And, finally, demand could drop, and grain companies might sell corn from the supplies they've accumulated. Conditions could improve, and they may want to rid themselves of high-priced corn that they may not need after all.

Regardless of what actually happens, you've decided you don't want to gamble or second-guess the future. You're happy with the current futures price and decide to sell (or price) your crop now, before it has actually been produced. You have two choices:

1. You can enter into a forward contract with a grain company. This contract is one between you and a grain processor or elevator. (This type of firm is known as a "commercial.") It will quote a price for your crop to be delivered to it at some future time, usually shortly after harvest. Often, the price is not as high as the market's current trading level.

2. As an alternative, you could sell your crop on the futures market. The futures markets are organized exchanges or marketplaces where many individuals congregate for buying and selling contracts in given markets for future delivery and/or speculation. Prices there are theoretically relatively free of manipulation by large commercial interests, which may have almost complete control over what you will be paid in your hometown area for your crop, if you choose option #1 above.

Provided your corn meets the proper exchange quality specifications, you can sell it in advance on the futures exchange. You won't get your money until the crop is delivered to the buyer, but the price you get is locked in. Regardless of where the price goes afterwards, you'll be guaranteed the price at which you sold your crop.

You could win or lose. If the cash market is higher by the time your crop is ready, you won't make as much as you might have had you waited. If the price is lower, then you are fortunate in having sold before the decline. Of course, you also have the option of doing nothing, hoping that corn will be much higher in the future. The essence of the futures market is, therefore, its use as a tool by which the producer and end user can hedge, or protect, profits. Futures are ideal hedges against rising or falling prices. The process by which producers hedge their risk is called "risk transfer."

■ What's in It for the Players?

Who takes the other side of the futures transaction, and why? In other words, who will buy the grain from you, why will they buy it, what will they do with it, and how will they sell it if they change their mind? Essentially, there are three categories of "players" in the futures game, as described in the following sections. Characteristics of these players are summarized in Figure 2.1.

Producers

These individuals and/or firms actually produce or process the commodity that is being traded. Whether it is silver, gold, petroleum, corn, live cattle, lumber, sugar, interest rates, stock indices, or currencies, producers are the ones who make the goods available, either by growing them, harvesting them, processing them, mining them, or lending them. Because they have a product they want to sell at a determined price, producers have to lock in costs. They may do this to guarantee a profit on an actual commodity they have on hand or have produced, or they may want to lock in a price on an item to avoid losing more money if the item is already declining.

Finally, producers may not have the goods at all. Rather, they may be protecting themselves from a possible side effect of declin-

---

■ **FIGURE 2.1** Participants in the Futures Markets and Their Usual Roles

Producers	Speculators	End Users
Sell to lock in profits	Buy or sell to make a profit but not to use the actual goods or products	Buy to use the product in their processing or business concern
May buy at times		
Usually farmers, banks, mining firms, manufacturers, etc.		May be sellers at times
	Often called "traders" (among other things)	May not actually use the goods they buy
Often called "hedgers"		
	Don't take delivery of the goods	
	Often trade for short-term swings	

ing or rising prices. For example, a jewelry store with considerable gold and silver jewelry on hand may fear a decline in the price of precious metals. It stands to lose money on its inventory as prices decline. Therefore, it may choose to sell futures contracts of silver and/or gold in expectation of the decline and thus has profited from the futures sale.

End Users

These are the individuals and/or firms that use the products sold by producers. They, too, have to lock in the cost of their production by the advance purchase of raw goods. Therefore, they either buy on the futures market or make a forward contract (previously defined). At times, the end user may become a seller rather than a buyer. Assume, for example, that too much of an item has been purchased or that the final product is not selling well; in such an event, the end user may switch to the sell side, implementing a "sell hedge" position.

The producer may at times switch sides as well. Assume that a firm has too little production to meet its obligations to others; in that case, the producer may then become a buyer rather than a seller. As you can see, roles in futures trading can change as a function of need, perceived need, supply, or demand.

Speculators

This is the largest group of futures traders in number. Speculators are sandwiched between the end users and the producers. They provide a buffer, although this is not their intended role. Perhaps no more than 1 to 3 percent of all futures contracts are actually completed by delivery, with the balance closed out before any actual exchange of goods occurs.

Speculators are often willing to assume the risk in markets at times and at prices that may not be attractive to the other two groups in the expectation of large percentage profit returns on price fluctuations. More details, including specifics of how futures contracts work, are provided later, as your understanding of basic concepts increases. What I want you to learn now are the concepts of futures trading. The basic issue is, of course, why trade?

■ Why Do Traders Trade?

At first glance, the answer to this question is obvious: traders trade to make profits. But there are many aspects to this simple answer. Let's look at a few of the most significant reasons for trading futures.

Futures trading requires relatively small start-up capital. Typically, one can get started in futures trading for as little as $10,000; and in some cases, even less capital is required. Many professionally managed trading pools require as little as $2,500 to $5,000 for participation. Although most traders aren't successful when starting with limited capital, this is one way to get your foot in the door. SSFs are, as you know, somewhat different from traditional futures because they require 20 percent margin. As such, more starting capital is required to trade a balanced portfolio of SSFs. A reasonable starting amount, although rather small, is $5,000.

Leverage is large. The typical futures contract can be bought or sold for 1 to 3 percent of its total value (margin). For example, a 100-troy-ounce gold contract at $400 per ounce ($40,000 cash value) requires about $1,500 to $2,000 in margin. The balance of the money will, of course, be due if and when the contract is completed (i.e., if you take delivery).

In the meantime, about $2,000 "controls" $40,000 in underlying value. In SSFs, the 20 percent margin allows less leverage than do traditional futures, but what you gain in more stability and less volatility compensates for the lower leverage. At 20 percent margin for SSFs, the leverage is still better than the usual 50 percent margin on stocks. Because this can work either for you or against you, your goal as a futures trader is to make leverage work in your favor.

Futures prices make relatively large moves. Futures prices fluctuate significantly almost daily. Some markets have the potential to return 100 percent or more per day on the required margin. Such leverage can work for or against you. Where there is great opportunity, there is often great risk as well. In SSFs, the volatility is often less substantial than in traditional futures because the margin requirement is larger. Volatility is often a function of margin and price magnitude.

Futures markets are highly liquid. By this I mean that it is possible to enter or exit a market quickly, which is not true with some individual stock and real estate investments. Some speculative stocks rarely trade; and real estate is often hard to dispose of quickly. With futures transactions, as with active stock transactions, one can enter and exit within seconds—which makes the futures market ideal for the speculator.

To maintain an orderly market in the specific securities they manage, there are dealers—known as market makers—in the securities exchange who buy and sell securities for their own account. The market maker system used in the SSF market maintains liquidity for buyers and sellers. It allows quick electronic processing of orders that adds to the liquidity of SSFs. And this inspires confidence in traders who want to use SSFs.

It's possible for virtually anyone to learn futures trading. In some areas of investment, you have to know either the right people or the right inside information. I previously noted that the effective use of fundamentals is not a simple task in the stock market. Even though correct inside information and fundamentals can be very helpful in trading futures, success doesn't depend exclusively on such information. There are few secrets to successful trading. Profitable trading is a skill that can be learned and can, in fact, be taught specifically, objectively, and successfully to those willing and able to learn. Virtually any individual with speculative capital, self-discipline, and the motivation to succeed has an opportunity in the futures markets—but it's not easy. It takes work and persistence. Furthermore, the SSF market is relatively new and requires experience above and beyond the simple understanding of traditional futures trading.

There are many SSFs. In addition to the traditional buy and sell short positions, many SSFs can be traded, and there will be more in the years ahead. In addition, there are narrow-based indexes (NBIs). These are discussed in Chapter 8.

Spreads can be used to increase the profit possibilities in SSFs. This will be explained in Chapter 9.

■ Understanding and Dealing with the Risk

You've all heard that there is considerable risk in futures trading, and there's no denying it. The statistics aren't in your favor when it comes to the traditional futures markets. It has been claimed that up to 95 percent of all traders lose their speculative money. How can *you* avoid becoming a statistic? Here are some ideas.

First and foremost, education is vital. It's important to know that the trader with a small amount of capital is most apt to lose because he can't play the game long enough to get into the highly profitable trades. The larger your starting amount, the more likely you are to be successful.

In addition, many time-tested principles exist that, if applied with consistency and discipline, will substantially improve your odds of success. Statistically, you can be wrong about the market more than 50 percent of the time and still make money, provided you limit your losses. Some of these principles are closing out losses quickly, not overtrading, limiting losses using stops, and diversification of positions.

It is the inability to keep losses small that makes most traders losers. You must keep losses small by following a precise trading system with discipline.

Furthermore, it is taking profits quickly and losses slowly that can make the statistics work against you. The successful trader is quick to limit losses. I will return to this point during the course of this book, as one of my goals is to teach you the proper philosophy (and effective actions) of trading in addition to the basics of the markets themselves. I am convinced that losses can be reduced by a significant degree if one learns how to limit risk, how to take losses quickly, and how to keep losses small.

Losses are part of every business. In retail or manufacturing businesses, for example, losses are made up of such things as rent, overhead, insurance, production costs, theft, and depreciation. Not all transactions are profitable, but they are the bottom line that differentiates the winners from the losers.

In the final analysis, risk is something each investor and trader must evaluate in relation to his or her financial situation. It is certain that more inherent risk exists in futures trading as it is commonly practiced today. However, without risk there can be no reward of the magnitude common in futures trading.

∎ The Concept of Risk Transfer

Perhaps the single most important concept to understand about futures trading, once the basics have been grasped, is that of *risk transfer*. If you are familiar with futures trading and fully understand its function as a vehicle for transferring risk, you need not read the following explanation. If, however you are unfamiliar with, or uncertain of, your knowledge, I urge you to read the several paragraphs below.

For every buyer of a futures contract there is a seller. The seller can be a speculator who is either liquidating a long position or establishing a new short position. If the seller is establishing a short position against a cash market position (i.e., the seller actually owns the product being sold), then the sell position is known as a *short hedge*. The seller has transferred the risk of his cash market position to the buyer of the futures contract.

The buyer in this case took a long position because he felt there was potential for the position to make money. The seller, on the other hand, wanted to protect his cash position from a potential decline. Each participant felt confident (or relatively confident) that he had the advantage: The seller has transferred the risk of holding a long cash position to the buyer; the buyer is speculating on the long side in the belief that a profit can be made. By now you must be thinking that one of these two market participants will be right and one absolutely has to lose money. Correct? No, not correct! Imagine the following scenario.

Trader 1 owns 100 ounces of gold, which is priced at $300/oz. Trader 1 believes, based on her information, that gold will decline to $250 per ounce at some point in the next six months. Accordingly, Trader 1 sells short a gold futures contract at $300/oz. Trader 2 has studied the charts and technical indicators as well as the fundamental situation in gold. He assumes, based on his studies, that gold could rise to $320/oz over the next few weeks. Accordingly, he acts on his expectations and buys gold futures at $300/oz.

A deal has now been struck. Trader 1 is short and Trader 2 is long. Gold begins to rise. Trader 1 has an open loss (i.e., her position is not closed out). Trader 2 is pleased because gold is now at $311, only $9 from his expected target. In a few days, gold reaches $320, and Trader 2 closes out his long position for a profit of $20, which on the 100 oz gold contract means $2,000 in actual cash profits. Trader 1 remains short. Her work indicates that gold will indeed decline. Several months pass, and gold declines to $265. Trader 1 elects to close out her short position, taking in a profit of $35/oz, or $3,500 in actual money.

As you can see, both participants can make money because they aren't the only ones in the game. There are thousands of other players. The risk of a position (long or short) can be passed on to any trader who can, in turn, pass the trade on to another trader. It is the liquidity of the marketplace that allows the risk transfer process to function effectively and at the same time allows speculators to take positions with the potential of profit. Because the futures market is a closed system, eventually someone must take the loss on the "hot potato," but the important factor is that the market provides the liquidity necessary for it to function.

Remember that the process of risk transfer does not require selling. Buyers who want to transfer the risk of not owning a given commodity can buy with the intention of taking delivery. Sellers can transfer risk because they have produced the given item (as in the case of a farmer or a mining company), or they can have an inventory of a given item that they intend to use in their production facility but wish to transfer the risk of a potential decline by using the futures market. Let's look briefly at a losing scenario, one in which the risk transfer works against the seller.

Trader 1 owns 1,000 barrels of crude oil that she wishes to hedge at $24 per barrel. She sells a futures contract against the cash position in anticipation of a decline to $20. If the decline occurs, she will have neutralized $4,000 in potential losses (i.e., the crude oil futures contract calls for 1,000 barrels of crude oil). However, the market does not cooperate. Crude oil rises to $28. Trader 1 closes out the short position at a loss.

■ How Single Stock Futures Differ from Traditional Futures

Futures trading in its traditional role has focused on such markets as grains, meats, metals, energies, financials, and tropicals (also known as "softs"). With the introduction of interest rate, currency, and stock index futures, the nature of the commodities markets changed dramatically. It is now possible to trade intangible items such as interest rates and stock indices. Other, more obscure futures markets such as Baltic freight futures, weather futures, and insurance futures have also paved the way for trading in SSFs.

But how does the SSF market differ from traditional futures trading? It differs in a number of ways. The biggest difference, in general, is the margin requirement. The margin requirement in the traditional futures market is from 1 percent to 10 percent of the underlying value of a commodity, depending on various conditions.

As an example, a 1,000 barrel contract of crude oil futures at a price of $28 per barrel would be worth $28,000 full value (i.e., $28 × 1,000 per barrel = $28,000). The margin on this contract might be about $1,500. The margin charged is determined by the specific exchange, which sets a minimum margin requirement. A brokerage house can charge more than the minimum but not less. In this case, the margin at 10 percent would be $2,800; at 5 percent it is $1,400. In other words, a small amount of money controls a large amount of a commodity; and this can work either for you or against you. It can increase your leverage (i.e., your ability to make a large amount of money on a small investment), or it can work against you if the market moves contrary to your position and erases your margin. In that case, you would be asked to post more margin or liquidate your position.

Single stock futures have a margin requirement of 20 percent as a minimum. This means that if you bought one contract of IBM futures with IBM at $80/share, the margin would be 20 percent of the full value of 100 shares, or 20 percent of $8,000 (that is, $1,600). As you can see, the leverage here is quite advantageous; you are able to control an $8,000 investment for only $1,600. If you bought the contract for 100 shares of IBM and the stock moved to $96 per share, the gain would be $1,600 on the futures contract as well as $1,600 in the stock. The return on your investment in the futures would be 100 percent on the futures contract. If you bought the stock on 50 percent margin then your return would be much less than the return on an SSF.

Remember that the SSF market has two distinct advantages over traditional futures: (1) Its larger margin requirements decrease volatility, and (2) stocks tend to be more stable than traditional futures. Both of these can work in favor of the trader.

Differences between Trading Stocks and Trading Futures

A futures contract has a limited life span, whereas a stock does not. It expires on a given date and must be closed out by the given date—win, lose, or draw. The underlying stock, however, can be kept indefinitely so long as you are willing to pay the interest on the margin and post more margin if the stock moves against you. Other significant differences exist as well between the purchase or short sale of a stock and the purchase or short sale of a single stock futures contract and will be discussed later.

There clearly are advantages well as disadvantages to trading in SSFs. In many cases, it's a question of "the bigger the front, the bigger the back," meaning the more significant the advantages, the more substantial can be the disadvantages. As with any financial vehicle, it is the trader or investor who must develop strategies and procedures for maximizing the advantages and minimizing the liabilities.

∎ Additional Uses of the Futures Markets

This chapter has so far briefly outlined preliminary concepts and applications of futures trading. Naturally, as a vehicle for speculating, hedging, or spreading risk, futures trading has significant importance. As a vehicle for stabilizing costs to producers and end users, futures trading is a vital tool.

SSF trading adds another facet to futures trading by merging futures and stocks. As I have pointed out previously, (and will tell you again), the SSF market opens a new era of trading to stock investors and traders and to futures traders. The ability to hedge a stock by selling an SSF is a highly effective tool for investors. Furthermore, the ability to spread stocks and NBIs against one another adds yet another vehicle to the storehouse of futures trading tools. Finally, the combined use of SSFs, stock options, and underlying stocks adds yet another level of applications. This is explained thoroughly in Chapter 9.

On a more pervasive level, however, an understanding of futures trading can prove very valuable to the investor not interested in actually trading futures. This book pays considerable attention to the hypothesis that a knowledge of futures price trends and futures market behavior can assist one in understanding economic trends as well as in forecasting the short-term to intermediate-term direction of prices. I also emphasize the fact that SSFs can be a lower-cost and potentially more effective way of participating in the equities markets. There are also long-range implications for investors who know how to use SSFs.

∎ Summary

Futures trading is a technique whereby one can buy and/or sell a variety of raw and processed commodity items, including financial instruments, stock indices, and SSFs, for anticipated delivery at some point in the future. The three major categories of participants in the futures markets, each with its own expectations, goals, and market methods, are producers, end users, and speculators. Futures trading allows producers and end users to lock in costs of production, thus improving economic stability as well as the stability of their particular business. In the case of SSFs, the producer or end user is the owner or holder of equities. Speculators are by far the largest category of traders and have no interest in making or taking delivery of products; their interest is playing market swings for profits.

Common objections to futures trading abound, some with merit, others unfounded. Some experts fear that the introduction of the SSF market will reduce trading in the underlying stocks and stock options. In practice, however, this has shown itself to be the opposite in markets where SSFs have traded longer than in the United States, such as in Spain.

Specific methods, systems, and procedures used in futures trading, a majority of which have been time tested, are designed to reduce its inherent risk. Even though futures trading involves considerable risk, this risk can be greatly reduced by consistent application of various principles. Futures trading can be an excellent vehicle for immense profit, or it can be a dangerous venture leading to financial ruin. Those who win often attribute their success to an attitude that reflects self-discipline, courage, consistency, persistence, effective trading techniques, and a willingness to learn from mistakes.

CHAPTER THREE

The History of Stock Trading: An Overview

■ The Origins of Stock Trading

Those who believe that the futures markets have been riddled with scandals are likely unaware that the history of stock trading in the United States was also grounded in scandals. Although the trading of shares in public companies did not originate in the United States, stock trading was very popular in America in the 1700s. At that time brokers gathered near Wall Street in Lower Manhattan to trade stocks alongside a 12-foot-high stockade. Although few (if any) formal rules and regulations governed stock trading, a radical change took place in 1798 as a result of a financial panic caused by William Duer. Duer had overextended his debts to several banks, which ultimately caused them to fail. Duer was sent to debtors' prison for his part in the financial debacle. To help prevent similar problems in the future, 24 brokers met to formalize a variety of trading rules known as the Buttonwood Agreement.

In the early 1800s, trading moved indoors with the formalization of the stock exchange as the New York Stock Exchange (NYSE) in

1863. Brokers who elected to remain outdoors to do their trading were forerunners of the American Stock Exchange (AMEX). Several periods of boom and bust occurred in the stock market since the mid-1800s, not the least of which was the crash of 1929.

As I noted before, trading in stocks was not without its heroes and villains nor its periods of boom and bust. Those who point a finger at futures trading as a manipulated or high-risk game need only examine some of the numerous stock scandals that have continued to haunt the equities markets since their inception to see that where there is risk and reward there also exists the potential for crime.

Stock trading remained essentially unchanged for many years other than the implementation of checks and balances to control market corners and stock manipulation. It was not until the introduction of stock index futures in 1982 that the game of stock trading was to change forever. Stock index futures improved the ability of money mangers, as well as individual investors and traders, to hedge their stock portfolios against baskets of stocks such as the S&P 500-stock index or the Value Line index. Although the introduction of stock index futures helped bring some degree of stability to the markets, it also helped usher in a new era of speculation that, in my view, resulted in a much more volatile stock market.

Now, with the introduction of SSFs, another level of speculation has been introduced, one that could easily jump market volatility to a new level. Yet in spite of this possibility, the fact remains that every investor now has the ability to protect himself further from market swings as well as the ability to participate in stock trading by posting a relatively small amount of money. This will bring more money into the game and, if the SSF market functions as many markets do, the small investor—who is usually undisciplined—will lose money while adding a buffer to the markets. Remember that a zero-sum game (ZSG) in futures markets is the key to understanding the basics of who wins and who loses and will be discussed further in future chapters.

■ The Traditional Role of Stocks as an Investment Vehicle

As you well know, stocks have long been considered the vehicle of choice for investors. Literally thousands of books and tens of thousands of Web sites purport to give investors and traders the information they need to be successful at stock investing. Whether one chooses to invest in stocks for the long haul or to day trade stocks with quick profits as the goal, a variety of strategies allow profits to be made. The simple buy low–sell high strategy is not the only one in which profits can be made. The various combinations of buying—and selling short—stocks, bonds, warrants, stock options, and LEAPS provide a variety of methods and procedures. LEAPs are long-term stock options. Buying a LEAP call option can give you the right to buy the underlying stock at a fixed price for up to one year as opposed to three or six months, which is the case in non-LEAP stock options. The stock investor has, until the introduction of SSFs, had numerous alternatives; and with the introduction of SSFs, the situation becomes both simpler and more complicated at the same time. Consider the possibilities that will eventually be open to traders and investors:

- You can buy an SSF contract with a smaller margin than you can buy a stock. This will open the markets to more traders, thereby increasing liquidity while providing a new client base to brokerage firms.
- You can sell short an SSF contract for a smaller margin than you can sell short an individual stock. Even though most investors and traders are averse to selling short, the vehicle to do so will be available to them.
- Selling short SSFs is easier than selling short stocks because there is no rule governing up ticks. As you may know, stock-trading regulations don't allow you to sell short a stock unless it has traded up from its last transaction. In a rapidly falling market, this could mean that your order won't get filled or will

be filled at a much more disadvantageous price than you had expected (on a market order). SSFs, on the other hand, don't have such a rule. Therefore, those who seek to establish short positions can do so more quickly.

- You can buy a stock and sell short an SSF contract against your position as a hedge.
- You can sell short a stock and buy an SSF contract against your position as a buy hedge.
- You can spread one stock against another. Say, for example, you think that United Airlines shares are likely to rise faster than American Airlines shares. You could buy United Airlines futures and sell short American Airlines futures, making money on the spread if your expectations are correct. (More about this later on.)
- You can buy a stock futures contract and hold it for delivery. In so doing, you would pay less money up front and pay no interest on the outstanding amount compared with paying interest on a stock margined at 50 percent in the traditional fashion.
- You could sell short a stock futures contract and wait to be called for delivery, thus being able to unload actual shares of stock that you own.
- You could use a combination of strategies employing SSFs, stock options, and/or stocks.
- You could combine LEAPS with SSFs for longer-term strategies, many of which are discussed in later chapters.

■ The New Role of Stocks as a Speculative Vehicle

Before the mid-1980s, when the major stock averages were much lower than they were in the late 1990s, stocks were considerably more stable and less speculative. However, with the lofty price levels achieved on the major stock averages and on individual stocks, speculative fever gripped stock markets all over the world. Intraday price swings became sufficiently large to attract short-term and day traders.

Combined with virtually instant electronic order execution and low commissions, stock markets the world over attracted more speculators and short-term traders than ever before. Adding to the speculative attraction of stocks in the 1990s and into the 2000s was the dramatic increase in trading volume. As Figure 3.1 shows, quarterly trading volume in 2002 was more than twice that in 1996 and more than seven times that in 1986.

Even the bear market that started in 2000 failed to diminish trading volume in the Dow Jones Industrial Average. Clearly, speculation in stocks is alive and well. As a further example of the large increase in trading volume, note the large increase in trading activity in the Nasdaq 100 Trust (QQQ) shares shown in Figure 3.2.

In spite of the fact that this market declined substantially from its year 2000 peak at over $120 per share to a low of just over $26 per share in 2002, trading volume jumped dramatically in 2001 and

■ **FIGURE 3.1** The Growth in Stock Trading Volume from 1986–2002. The vertical bars show total share volume.

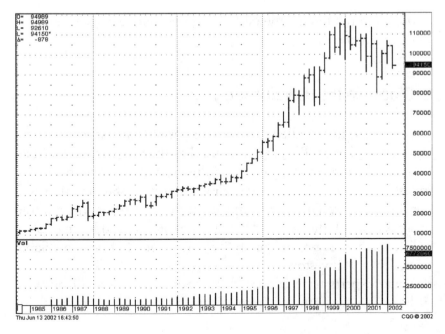

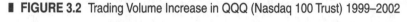

■ FIGURE 3.2 Trading Volume Increase in QQQ (Nasdaq 100 Trust) 1999–2002

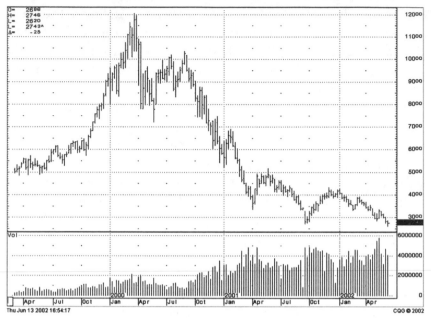

2002, again reinforcing the underlying speculative activity and liquidity of stocks.

■ Stocks in the New Economy

Although the so-called new economy was dealt a severe blow by the bear market of 2000, the odds are that the new economy will be revived when technology once again regains its luster as an area for investors. Stock investing and trading are here to stay, and they will continue to play a major role in the future. Given the integral role of stocks in both the new and the old economy, the addition of SSFs will help to increase the variability and range of choices available to traders and investors.

Some experts have expressed concerns that the availability of SSFs will dissuade traders from selecting stocks as their vehicle of choice. This has, in fact, not been the case in markets where SSF trading was introduced before its availability in the United States.

Increased Stock Market Volatility, Day Trading, and SSFs

Because of the lower margin requirement for futures, price moves in futures tend to be more volatile and more exaggerated than they are in stocks, particularly on an intraday basis. Day trading activity and interest reached its peak with the top of the bull market in 2000. The addition of SSFs now allows day traders another vehicle for their activities, one that allows them more intricate strategies. Stock day traders will find the leverage in SSFs more advantageous, whereas futures day traders will find more vehicles for their day trading activities. Rather than being restricted to day trading in five or six active futures markets, futures day traders now have a wide variety of vehicles at their disposal.

■ The New Era of Risk and Reward

Clearly the introduction of SSFs now offers many possibilities to stock and futures traders. Although this new vehicle will create many opportunities, it will also bring with it dangers. Traders who lack discipline, organization, and effective trading strategies will be net losers in the new game, whereas professionals who follow a definitive plan implemented with discipline and consistency will emerge as winners. There is no substitute for education and self-discipline. The new era of risk and reward will, as always, be a two-sided situation. I hope the lessons and caveats offered in this book will tilt the advantage in your favor.

CHAPTER FOUR

The Basics of Stock and Futures Trading

This chapter is intended primarily for those who are either unfamiliar with the basics of stock and futures trading or feel the need to freshen their understanding in one or both areas. Because this book will appeal to several levels of investors and traders, it needs to include at the outset the most basic information.

■ How Stock Trading Works

The modern method of stock trading is significantly different from the specialist system that has been in use for many years. Even though many stocks are still traded in the old way, the specialist system is rapidly fading, eventually to be replaced by fully electronic trading that uses market maker firms. A middleman will still be there, but the process will be fully transparent, which will decrease the tricks and unfair price fills.

The traditional method of stock trading at the New York Stock Exchange (NYSE) relied on the specialist as a facilitator of transactions. A given specialist or specialist firm would be responsible for making a market (i.e., maintaining) in a given stock or stocks. The specialist firm is responsible for maintaining a book or inventory of these given stocks in order to provide an orderly (if possible) base of transactions in the stocks by balancing buy and sell orders.

Specialists maintain an inventory of shares and, when demand is strong, draw from the inventory, raising prices to balance the orders and make money for their own efforts. When there is an oversupply of sellers, specialists mark prices down and take in stock, holding it in inventory in order to sell it at a higher price when demand returns. This is, of course, a simplification of the process. And although many have criticized this system as archaic, unfair, or even manipulated, the system worked for many decades. This system is slowly being replaced by fully electronic procedures, as noted previously. The SSF market is fully electronic.

■ Investing, Trading, and Speculating

I'd first like to define, at least in general terms, the distinctions between investing, trading, and speculating, as I'll be referring to these activities throughout the book.

Investing is the act of buying an object, a piece of property, or a security for the longer term. Generally, I consider any purchase that one intends to keep for at least a year to be an investment. More often than not, however, investments tend to be held for many years in anticipation of large price appreciation as well as tax benefits. The term *security* suggests that purchases for the longer term are safe. The term may very well be a misnomer given the fact that stocks once considered secure have shown themselves to be anything but that. *Equities* is actually a more appropriate term. This is not to say there are no relatively safe stocks or bonds, but the degree of risk in all investments has increased substantially since the early 1970s and in particular since the early 1990s. Nevertheless, an investment is a longer-term proposition that investors expect will eventually yield profits. Investors tend to act slowly, to add to their investment if prices decline (assuming they have the money and the confidence in the securities they own), and to buy investments that will also yield dividends.

Traders, on the other hand, are an entirely different breed. Their raison d'etre (or, as the French would say, their reason for existence) is simply to capitalize on relatively short-term price movements up and down. Whereas the investor is primarily a buyer who intends to hold positions for a longer period of time, the trader is willing to take long as well as short positions for brief periods of time.

Traders (also called speculators) have been frowned on as mercenary, ruthless, disinterested in anything but money, and opportunistic. Yet historically they have provided the liquidity that helps investors find a ready market when they sell and when they buy. Furthermore, traders are often like hedge funds, whose goal is to minimize their exposure and maximize their profits by trading for the short term from the long side as well as the short side. In effect, traders are speculators as opposed to investors.

Finally, and by no means of lesser importance, is the *day trader*. As the daily trading ranges in stocks have increased, as commissions have declined, and as electronic trading has allowed virtually instantaneous execution of trades, day trading has grown by leaps and bounds. My three books on day trading—*The Compleat Day Trader*, *The Compleat Day Trader II*, and *The Compleat Guide to Day Trading Stocks* (*compleat* is defined as "highly accomplished")—were bestsellers when day trading was in its heyday. But this all changed in early 2000 when stock markets topped.

This doesn't mean that day trading has ceased to exist or that it doesn't provide liquidity to the markets. It simply means that in the environment of the year 2002, it is not nearly so easy to make money as a day trader in comparison with how easily day traders could make money from 1997 through 2000.

The day trader is a speculator, not an investor, and as such is the ultimate market mercenary. The day trader in stocks is more often a buyer than a seller for the simple reason that in order to execute a short sale, an uptick from the last trade is required. When stocks decline in a virtual free fall, the day trader cannot easily execute a trade at a good price and is therefore somewhat limited in profit potential.

Figure 4.1 more clearly illustrates the market participants in stocks. To a certain extent this figure also applies to the traditional futures markets but not in exactly the same way. The reasons for making these distinctions between market participants are these:

- Investors can use SSFs as a vehicle for protecting their current investment positions in the event of market moves against their positions. In the past they could only do so by using stock options or liquidating their positions.
- Hedge funds (pending approval by regulatory agencies) can use futures as their trading vehicle for speculative positions, spreads, and hedges against existing portfolios rather than being restricted to stocks themselves, which would require a higher margin requirement.
- Day traders in stocks can use SSFs for quick moves without the need to post as much margin as stocks would require
- Short-term traders can use SSFs instead of stocks, thereby gaining more leverage because of the lower margin requirement

I FIGURE 4.1 This chart shows how different market participants in the stock market are oriented in different time frames.

Market Category

Investors	Traders	Day Traders
Pension funds	Hedge funds	Hedge funds
Individual investors	Individual investors	Individual investors
Mutual funds	Short-term traders	Floor brokers
Brokers	Mutual funds	Market makers
Retirement funds	Some banks	Arbitrageurs
Banks	Floor brokers	
	Market makers	

Long Term . . . Intermediate Term . . . Short Term . . . Intraday

Time Frame

- Short-term traders can use SSFs for short-term spreads and as hedges against existing short-term positions in stocks. This will be explained more fully in Chapter 9.

And there will likely be many more applications once traders and investors become comfortable with the functioning and behavior of the SSF market.

■ The Intent and Use of Margin

As you know, margin is the "down payment" you make on a stock purchase. Whereas the margin on stocks is actually a down payment on the full amount, the use of margin in futures contracts is quite different. If you use margin for stocks, your broker charges you daily interest on the amount borrowed. Even though this doesn't seem to be an especially large cost, it does add up; and when combined with commissions, the total costs can often eat up the profits generated by short-term traders.

In futures trading, on the other hand, there is no daily interest charge. The margin money is, in effect, a down payment but one with no interest charge. This feature alone makes the SSF market very attractive to short-term traders.

■ Online Trading in Stocks

Online trading in stocks has been growing by leaps and bounds since the late 1990s, but this has not been the case with most traditional futures markets. In fact, the U.S. futures markets have been slow to catch up. On the other hand, fully electronic trading at the LIFFE exchange in London and the Eurex exchange in Europe has been viable for several years.

For many years the "good old boy" network of floor brokers (pit traders) in futures opposed the fully electronic market because it threatened their income. In the past, pit brokers could buy at wholesale prices from the public while selling at retail prices and vice versa by offering to buy at prices lower than the prevailing price and offering to sell at prices higher than the prevailing price. In a rising market they played their game, often with great success when the trading public sold or bought positions at the market. By skillfully judging the market to get the "edge," the pit brokers could buy at a given price and sell almost immediately at a slightly higher price. In addition, they could often sell short at a high price and cover their short positions quickly at a lower price. In effect, the floor broker served as the middle person.

Although the mandate of the floor broker in futures was to provide liquidity and make for an orderly market, doubts have risen about the validity of this mandate as trading volume and liquidity have increased. The purpose of the market specialist in stocks has also been, purportedly, to provide liquidity and make for an orderly market. Yet questions have risen here too about whether specialists and pit brokers actually served their supposed purpose. With the advent of fully electronic trading, it has become clear that the historical role of the floor broker is no longer a necessity. The role of the floor broker in futures trading is slowly being replaced by electronic trading platforms, in which buy and sell orders are matched through approved market makers.

An example of a fully electronic SSF market is one run by the OneChicago organization, a joint venture of the Chicago Board of Trade, the Chicago Mercantile Exchange, and the Chicago Board Options Exchange. The NQLX in New York also trades SSFs. Orders are matched by computer, thereby giving market participants the best possible execution of their trades at the fastest possible speed. As of the date of writing, approximately 16 exchanges throughout the world trade about 300-plus SSFs. Experience has shown these markets to be efficient and viable.

■ Time Perspectives and Goals

Of the distinct differences between investors, traders, and pure speculators, the essential differences are time based. In other words, investors have a lengthy, or extended, time perspective, whereas traders have a considerably shorter time frame. Because futures contracts have a defined life span (usually one to three years), their use may be more suited to the short term and day traders than to investors. However, for investors who seek to protect a long position in stocks, the possibility of selling short SSFs against a long stock position, even for a limited period, offers a great advantage.

■ Narrow-Based Indexes (NBIs)

Narrow-based indexes are SSFs that represent an industry group. Just as the S&P 500 index represents 500 stocks, an NBI may represent only 5 stocks in a given industry. The SSF market has listed a number of NBIs for trading, as shown in Figure 4.2. Additional NBIs will be added as the SSF market grows.

▌ FIGURE 4.2 Narrow-Based Indexes Listing (as of March 14, 2002)

Airlines
AMR Corp./Del (AMR)
Continental Airlines Inc.–Class B
(CAL)
Delta Air Lines (DAL)
Southwest Airlines (LUV)
UAL Corp. (UAL)

Biotech
Amgen Inc. (AMGN)
Biogen Inc. (BGEN)
Chiron Corp. (CHIR)
Genzyme Corp.–Gen'l Division
(GENZ)
Human Genome Sciences (HGSI)

Computers
Apple Computer Inc. (AAPL)
Dell Computer Corp. (DELL)
International Business Machines
(IBM)
Research in Motion (RIMM)
Sun Microsystems (SUNW)

Defense
General Dynamics (GD)
Lockheed Martin (LMT)
Northrop Grumman Corp. (NOC)
Raytheon Co. (RTN)

Investment Banking
Goldman Sachs Group, Inc. (GS)
Lehman Brothers Holdings (LEH)
Merrill Lynch & Co., Inc. (MER)
Morgan Stanley Dean Witter &
Co. (MWD)

Oil Services
Baker Hughes Inc. (BHI)
BJ Services (BJS)
Halliburton Co. (HAL)
Schlumberger Ltd. (SLB)
Weatherford International (WFT)

Retail
Autozone Inc. (AZO)
Best Buy Co., Inc. (BBY)
Circuit City Stores (CC)
Home Depot Inc. (HD)
Wal-Mart Stores Inc. (WMT)

Semiconductor Components
Broadcom Corp.–Class A (BRCM)
Intel Corp. (INTC)
Micron Technology Inc. (MU)
Texas Instruments (TXN)
Xilinx Inc. (XLNX)

CHAPTER FIVE

Synthesis: The Marriage of Stocks and Futures

The union of stocks and futures into the single stock futures contract brings to the financial markets a new vehicle as well as a new era in trading and investing. By combining the lower margin of futures with the wide range of available stocks and narrow-based indices, a new area of financial possibilities is open to investors and traders. But to fully appreciate and use the SSF market to its maximum potential, a thorough understanding of its functioning is necessary. This chapter provides the needed facts.

■ Examining the Single Stock Futures Contract

The current SSF contract had its roots in the Universal Stock Futures that were first traded at the LIFFE exchange in London. SSF trading was slow to come to the United States but adopted quickly in many other countries following their success in London.

Which Stocks Are Traded as SSFs?

As of March 14, 2002, OneChicago, the joint venture that created SSF trading in the United States, listed the following 70 SSFs. SSFs are based on individual stocks, whereas an NBI is one index based on a group of stocks within the same industry.

American Express Co. (AXP)
American International Group
   Inc. (AIG)
Amgen Inc. (AMGN)
AMR Corp./Del (AMR)
AOL Time Warner Inc. (AOL)
Applied Materials (AMAT)
AT&T Corp. (T)
Bank Of America Corp. (BAC)
Bank One Corp. (ONE)
Best Buy Co., Inc. (BBY)
Biogen Inc. (BGEN)
Bristol-Myers Squibb Co. (BMY)
Broadcom Corp.–Class A (BRCM)
Brocade Communications Sys.
   (BRCD)
Cephalon Inc. (CEPH)
Check Point Software Tech.
   (CHKP)
ChevronTexaco Corp. (CVX)
Cisco Systems Inc. (CSCO)
Citigroup Inc. (C)
Coca-Cola Co. (KO)
Dell Computer Corp. (DELL)
eBay Inc. (EBAY)
EMC Corp. (EMC)
Emulex Corp. (EMLX)
Exxon Mobil Corp. (XOM)
Ford Motor Co. (F)

General Electric Co. (GE)
General Motors Corp. (GM)
Genzyme Corp.–Gen'l Division
   (GENZ)
Goldman Sachs Group, Inc. (GS)
Halliburton Co. (HAL)
Home Depot Inc. (HD)
Idec Pharmaceuticals Corp.
   (IDPH)
Intel Corp. (INTC)
International Business Machines
   (IBM)
InVision Technologies Inc.
   (INVN)
J.P. Morgan Chase & Co. Inc.
   (JPM)
Johnson & Johnson (JNJ)
KLA-Tencor Corp. (KLAC)
Krispy Kreme Doughnuts Inc.
   (KKD)
Merck & Co. Inc. (MRK)
Merrill Lynch & Co. Inc. (MER)
Micron Technology Inc. (MU)
Microsoft Corp. (MSFT)
Morgan Stanley Dean Witter &
   Co. (MWD)
Motorola Inc. (MOT)
Newmont Mining Corp. Hldg Co.
   (NEM)

Nokia Corp. ADR* (NOK)

Northrop Grumman Corp. (NOC)

Novellus Systems Inc. (NVLS)

Oracle Corp. (ORCL)

PepsiCo Inc. (PEP)

Pfizer Inc. (PFE)

Philip Morris Cos. Inc. (MO)

Procter & Gamble Co. (PG)

QLogic Corp. (QLGC)

QUALCOMM, Inc. (QCOM)

SBC Communications Inc. (SBC)

Schlumberger Ltd. (SLB)

Siebel Systems, Inc. (SEBL)

Sprint Corp.-PCS Group (PCS)

Starbucks Corp. (SBUX)

Sun Microsytems Inc. (SUNW)

Symantec Corp. (SYMC)

Texas Instruments Inc. (TXN)

Tyco International Ltd. (TYC)

UAL Corp. (UAL)

VERITAS Software Corp. (VRTS)

Verizon Communications Inc.
  (VZ)

Wal-Mart Stores Inc. (WMT)

*American Depositary Receipt

■ How SSFs Work

The SSF concept is, as you can see, very simple. You can buy or sell a futures contract on any of the listed stocks or narrow-based indices. The futures contract has a given delivery date on which it expires or ends. As long as the contract has not expired and there is sufficient trading volume to allow transactions, you can buy back a short position or sell out a long position either at the prevailing price or at a specific price.

At the risk of overstating the obvious, I remind you that if you close out your short position at a lower price than the one at which you sold it, you make a profit. If you close out a long position at a higher price than the one at which you bought it, you make a profit. The reverse holds true for losses.

The SSF contract does not "decay" over time as stock options do. It is tied directly to the price of the stock and fluctuates with it accordingly. If the underlying stock rises, then the futures contract rises. If the underlying stock declines, then the futures contract declines. You can spread one SSF against another (to be discussed later) and make money on the spread or lose money on the spread as a function of the movement in the underlying stocks.

■ Regulations

The SSF market has its own unique set of rules and regulations determined by the government and professional agencies that oversee trading such as the National Futures Association (NFA), the Securities and Exchange Commission (SEC), and the Commodity Futures Trading Commission (CFTC). These rules are readily available from your broker or the agencies themselves. I strongly recommend that you familiarize yourself with these regulations, at least in general terms, to avoid violations. Because these rules and regulations change over time, I suggest you check the current state of information before you begin trading in SSFs.

■ Margin and Delivery Considerations

Margin requirements for SSFs are 20 percent of the underlying value of 100 shares of the stock. Therefore, a stock trading at $50 per share would have a total value of $5,000 for 100 shares. The 100-share SSF contract's full value would be $5,000 and the margin required to trade the contract would be 20 percent of the $5,000, or $1,000. Regulatory agencies have the right to increase the trading margin on any given SSF as a function of various underlying conditions.

The agencies may decide to increase the margin on a given SSF if trading activity becomes too volatile or if the price of an SSF contract increases too rapidly or declines too rapidly. The purported intent of raising margins is to decrease speculative activity. In rare circumstances, regulatory agencies in the futures markets have imposed a "liquidation only" ruling in given markets in order to decrease excessive volatility and speculation.

Each futures market has precise contract specifications that define important trading details. You would do best to check with your broker to make certain that you have closed out your SSF position prior to delivery unless, of course, you want to take delivery of the underlying stock(s) or their cash equivalent.

■ The Mechanics of Trading SSFs

Because the SSF market is electronic, orders can be filled in a matter of seconds. Here is how the order flow in an SSF works: You place your order through your broker or from your computer through an online entry system. Your order goes to the electronic order-matching computer. The order-matching computer matches your order with orders of other traders and market makers in the system. Once matched, your order fill is reported back to you. The SSF market is "fully transparent," which means that the possibility of price manipulation is small.

The OneChicago exchange uses advanced computer technology to enable their electronic trading system for SSFs. The trading process begins with a trader's order entry and ends with electronic distribution and reporting of trade status and confirmation, clearing, and back-office processing of the trade following the general outline described earlier. Whether you enter your trade through an electronic terminal or through a broker who then enters the order for you, the process is the same.

The SSF market as traded at OneChicago provides traders with a choice of trading platforms that are designed to simplify the order entry and execution process. The platforms are structured in a fashion that makes use of the systems and training that individuals and brokerage firms already have in place.

Most brokers are already online with OneChicago either via the CBOEdirect platform (Chicago Board Options Exchange) or GLOBEX (24-hour trading platform at the Chicago Mercantile Exchange), new SSF investors can often begin trading at OneChicago immediately.

Some traders and/or brokerage firms may want to incorporate specific features in their interface with the OneChicago SSF market. The exchange, therefore, offers numerous front-end trading platforms for both CBOEdirect and GLOBEX. Among these are a variety of broker-specific systems, proprietary systems for various trading firms, and independent software vendor (ISV) platforms, as well as CBOEdirect workstations and GLOBEX Trader workstations. Each individual or firm can decide on the platform that best serves their purpose.

The "Match Engine"

As noted earlier, your order once entered is matched with the orders of other traders, so as to effect a fair and equitable price execution. This process is completed by a computerized system (i.e., software) called a "match engine." OneChicago uses the CBOEdirect match engine for electronic trading, which can accommodate large trading volume demands during highly active trading periods. The OneChicago match engine is designed to work with the Lead Market Maker system, which provides a liquid, dynamic trading environment. This means that SSF orders can be executed quickly, at a fair price to the buyer and the seller, regardless of how heavy trading volume may be.

For more information on this process, I recommend a visit to the OneChicago Web site at the following address: <www.onechicago .com/index.html>. This location will also provide you with up-to-date information on contract specifications, delivery dates, contract settlement, and a variety of other relevant topics. The Lead Market Maker system is vital to the effective functioning of SSFs. It behooves all SSF traders to understand the Lead Market Maker system.

CHAPTER SIX

Aspects of Fundamentals

Let's begin by exploring a basic controversy of futures trading (this book challenges many concepts and beliefs revered by a majority of speculators) by looking at what I call the "good, the bad, and the ugly": fundamentals, technicals, and the peculiar offspring of their marriage that one might, for public relations purposes, term *eclectics*. I begin with a critical overview of the two major approaches to futures trading and then examine their hybrid to see which, if any, might be the most desirable for SSF trading. My views, right or wrong, valid or invalid, are designed to stimulate thought and, in so doing, promote positive change. Opinions are plentiful, but opinions based on considerable experience should not be dismissed lightly.

■ Fundamental Analyses

What is a "fundamental"? Do we mean fundamental as opposed to trivial or fundamental in the sense of basic or fundamental in the sense of a building block? Let's look at a recent definition of the term as found in *Futures Trading: Concepts and Strategies* (NYIF, 1988): "Fundamental analysis . . . is based on a study of the underlying supply and demand factors that are likely to shape the trend of prices."

Fundamentalists use historic economic information and current statistics to establish a supply and demand price forecast. They then relate estimates of this year's supply and demand balance to the historical price to decide if the current price is too high, too low, or just right. To arrive at an estimate of this year's supply, fundamentalists examine historical reports of such things as costs, earnings, inventories, order backlogs, corporate management, foreign exchange rates, interest rates, etc.

Fundamentalists also look at the impact of competition from substitutes or new products. They monitor changes in consumption patterns and per capita income affecting demand. This list would have to be extended significantly to include all the primary determinants of price; yet the accuracy of the current price evaluation would depend on the accuracy of the estimates and the weighting of factors. Don't think, though, that because of the complexity of the information involved, that fundamental methods are too complex to be of value. Econometric formulas that use computers can reduce this mass of data sufficiently to provide adequate information for trading and investing purposes.

The difficulty with the fundamentalists' approach for most speculators is that vast amounts of time and money can be consumed to obtain the past and present data and to work them into reliable formulations. To continue to update these data each day would be the task of a full-time staff. (Time-sharing computer services, which provide this information, are equally expensive.) The individual trader who wishes to use the fundamental approach is in direct competition with the largest professional traders in the world, who have huge resources of information and analysis. In such a competition, the outcome is not often a surprise; professionals usually win.

Fundamentals, then, are the economic realities that ultimately affect price, and fundamentalists are those who somehow formulate a trading plan or trading approach on the basis of fundamentals. In other words, fundamentalists use the basics of supply and demand to determine whether prices should increase or decrease. On the basis of these expectations, they make buy and sell decisions.

The good news about using fundamentals as a trading or invest-ing tool is that they reflect the true underlying supply and demand conditions for a given stock or futures market. Yet the limitation of fundamentals in SSF trading is that they are often known first pri-marily to professional traders as opposed to the general public. Furthermore, it is often difficult, if not impossible, for any individ-ual or group of traders to be aware of all important fundamentals at any given time.

Fundamental analysis has its roots in economics, and just as there are many economic theories, so too are there many different ap-proaches to fundamental analysis. The common element in all these approaches is the study of the purported causes of price in-creases and price decreases in the hope that the fundamentalists will be able to ascertain changes before they occur. Their success rests on the availability of accurate assessments of the variables they analyze, as well as on the availability of variables that may not be known to other fundamental analysts. Because the surplus of statis-tics available to fundamentalists at any given point can be over-whelming, fundamentalists must be selective and prepared to evaluate a massive amount of data. There are many different types of fundamentalists, who evaluate different types of data at different times. Some, by virtue of their skill and expertise, can provide ac-curate forecasts, whereas others, working with the same tools, make worthless forecasts.

■ Shortcomings of Fundamental Analysis

The popularity of computer technology has, unfortunately, over-shadowed the excellent work being done by many individual re-searchers in the area of fundamental analysis. The tendency of modern society to look for quick and easy solutions to problems has been partially responsible for the shift away from the implementa-tion of fundamental analysis. On the other hand, the difficulty and complexity of fundamental analysis have, in part, stimulated the contemporary trend toward simpler solutions.

The average individual has very limited success in understand-ing, analyzing, and implementing massive amounts of fundamental statistics. Even if all the relevant statistics were available, the average individual would have difficulty interpreting their meaning in relation to futures trading, which is, in essence, timing. Some of the difficulties with fundamental analysis can be summarized as follows:

- Not all fundamentals about stocks or futures can be known at any given time. Some only become known to the trading public after it is too late to act on the information.
- The importance of different fundamentals varies at different times. It is difficult to know which fundamentals are most significant at which time. To know this you must be highly experienced as well as informed.
- The average speculator may have difficulty gathering and interpreting the wealth of information that is available for every market. In fact, with the advent of the Internet, most traders suffer from information overload that can be confusing and frustrating.
- Fundamental analysis often fails to answer the important question that faces most speculators—the question of timing. Exactly when to take action is a critically important issue especially in the SSF market.
- Most fundamental statistics are available after the fact. By the time they are gathered by various government agencies or reporting services throughout the world, they are often old information and don't necessarily reflect the immediate situation. (See also the first point above.)
- Fundamentals can be significantly altered by such abrupt changes as government actions, weather, politics, international events, and certain technical factors. It may take time for these items to be reflected in fundamental statistics.
- The effort and cost involved in gathering, updating, and interpreting fundamental data may not, in the long run, yield cost-effective results. The cost of maintaining a complete, current, and accurate fundamental database is prohibitive to the average trader or investor.
- Most fundamental analysis doesn't provide alternatives based on price behavior but instead provides alternatives based on

changes in underlying conditions. These changes may be so slow that no visible or perceptible alterations in bullish or bearish stance can be justified when, in fact, a major change in a trend may have begun. Failure to recognize the new trend early in its inception can be very costly.

Yet in spite of these shortcomings, fundamental analysis still has its place in the commodities world. Ultimately, the price of every commodity is a function of fundamentals. Unfortunately, fundamental analysis has been the whipping boy of market technicians for many years now and, whether justified or not, has led to an understatement of its importance.

Rest assured that the fundamentals are very important, and their implementation can yield significant results over the long term for investors. I maintain that fundamental analysis has its place for the intermediate-term and long-term trader; for the short-term speculator in SSFs, however, fundamentals are unlikely to yield the sought-after results. The individual who is willing to establish a major position and possibly add to the position slowly over time can do very well. This is the proper place for the fundamentalist.

Typically, individuals employed to provide price forecasts, hedging patterns, purchasing programs, and planning programs for commercial end users or suppliers are especially good at understanding and implementing fundamentals. Because these individuals are not primarily concerned with timing, they frequently ride through virtually any storm. Speculators, however, cannot use the same approach because their capital, time, patience, and tolerance are limited by available resources. At 20 percent margin, the risk of holding a losing position too long is substantial.

■ Applying Fundamentals

Fundamental analysis is not the curse many contemporary traders consider it. To be even unexpected, international events are ultimately reflected in fundamental statistics that forecast price levels and direction, but response time can be slow. Unfortunately, the interpretation of fundamentals is both a science and an art that most specu-lators and average futures traders have difficulty implementing. The experience and knowledge that are especially important in analyzing and implementing fundamentals cannot be acquired as quickly as can the experience and knowledge necessary in technical analysis.

If you are still interested in the application of fundamentals, I suggest that you take the following advice to heart before you at-tempt to apply your knowledge to the SSF market:

- Study economics thoroughly. Acquaint yourself with various microeconomic and macroeconomic theories, particularly as they apply to production and consumption. Learn how stock trends are influenced by changes in economic conditions.
- Acquire a thorough knowledge of the production, consump-tion, critical factors, and implementation of the markets, stocks, or industry groups (NBIs) you wish to trade.
- Attempt to specialize. There are so many factors to consider that you cannot keep abreast of all SSFs and all economic trends, even with the aid of a computer. Therefore, you might want to specialize in one or two groups of markets (e.g., air-lines, metals, health care).
- Plan to spend several years learning to apply fundamentals. This is a highly complex field, one not mastered easily. Once mastered, however, the benefits can be substantial for the intermediate-term and long-term trader (i.e., investor).

∎ How to Select the Important Fundamentals

Which fundamentals are important is clearly a matter of percep-tion. Virtually any fact or factor can be considered important in the fundamental analysis of SSFs; and the fundamentals that affect the underlying stock will also affect the SSF for that stock. In the case of traditional commodities trading, markets such as wheat are af-fected by such fundamentals as, among others, weather, crop condi-tions, imports, exports, crop size domestically and in other producing nations, economic trends, supply, demand, competing products, and interest rates.

Fundamentals in stocks are equally many and varied; and some are more important than others at different times. Although the earnings of a given stock are important at all times, this fundamental can easily be overshadowed by the resignation of a CEO, by an investigation, or by the news of a merger or new product line. Investor and trader perceptions play a very important role in the price movement of stocks and futures. Fundamentals that may have been important last week may no longer be important this week. Clearly, investor and trader psychology play a key role in the price movement of stocks and SSFs (an important topic discussed more thoroughly in Chapter 13).

News as a Fundamental

Perhaps the most important short-term fundamental factor affecting the price of futures and stocks is the news. The news to which I refer can come in many different forms and disguises. As in the case of pure fundamentals, news can be interpreted by investors in a variety of ways. As an example, consider the following scenario. On June 27, 2002, Motorola announced that it would lay off 7,000 employees. At the same time it announced that it would meet its current earnings projections. To the casual observer, the news of a 7,000-employee layoff sounded grim. Common logic suggested that if the company had to lay off 7,000 employees, business must be terrible and the stock price would likely decline. Yet this quick conclusion failed to take into consideration that Motorola has over 100,000 employees worldwide and that by decreasing its employee census by 7,000, the company would lower its overhead and therefore gain more operating capital. In the short run the news seemed negative, but in the long run it suggested an aggressive intent by management to improve earnings on the bottom line. Whereas the average investor would have expected Motorola shares to decline in price, they rose because the news was actually bullish rather than bearish.

The Motorola scenario is only one minor example of how the news can affect markets, as any seasoned trader or investor knows. No one disagrees that news affects markets, but the manner in which the news can be used for trading is a function of individual trading style and methodology. Many experienced traders take positions contrary to that expected by novices on the basis of the news, because news is generally already factored into the price of a market by the time it has been made public. The old adage "Buy the rumor, sell the news" is well worth remembering. Simply stated, this dictum tells us that trading contrary to the news may be more profitable than reacting to the news. In the SSF market, the ability to trade contrary to the news may be one of the best strategies.

Reaction and Overreaction to the News

Because the news is often viewed in different ways by different traders, the impact on SSF price trends can be varied. *What appears to be good news may actually be bad news, and what appears to be bad news may actually be good news.* This is often what the novice trader or investor finds so confusing about the markets. And this is often what accounts for emotional decisions that result in losses.

News that is unexpected or significantly different from what was expected often results in a dramatic overreaction by investors and traders. Whereas the general public tends to respond to such news emotionally, professional traders frequently take advantage of such overreactions by trading contrary to the news. When the majority of traders respond to news by overreacting on the sell side, professional traders buy. When the majority of traders respond to bullish news by overreacting on the buy side, professional traders often take short positions. Such instances of excessive exuberance or excessive pessimism in response to news are the lifeblood of seasoned short-term and day traders.

As an example of such overreactions, consider the phenomenon of the "opening price gap" in futures and stock trading. An *opening price gap up* occurs when a market opens its day session above the high of the previous day. More often than not, such opening price gaps up occur as an overreaction to very bullish news. An *opening price gap down* occurs when a market opens its day session below the low of the previous day. More often than not, opening price gaps down occur as an overreaction to very bearish news.

Opening gaps such as these tend to reverse themselves by the end of the trading session. In other words, an opening price gap down can easily reverse itself, resulting in an up move rather than a down move, whereas an opening price gap up can frequently reverse itself to result in a down move rather than an up move. This happens because professional traders take advantage of the news to establish positions contrary to the direction of the opening price gap *if* the given market can trade back into the price range of the previous day. This approach can be used by itself as a systematic trading method for day trades and is described more fully in my book *The Compleat Guide to Day Trading Stocks* (McGraw-Hill, 2000). Three examples of how gap openings in reaction to news can yield significant profitable opportunities in the opposite direction are shown in Figures 6.1, 6.2, and 6.3.

As you can see from the foregoing illustrations, emotional selling and emotional buying cause opening price gaps to occur. Typically, following the opening gap, prices move in the opposite direction. (More about this aspect of market emotion later.)

■ How Stock Fundamentals Affect Underlying SSF Price Trends

Fundamentals impact investor and trader perceptions and motivate actions. As a result of changes in fundamental conditions, investors and traders either buy or sell stocks, or they add to their existing positions. Because the underlying trend for SSFs is a function of the underlying trend in stocks, the two markets move together a vast majority of the time. On occasion, the SSF market may be somewhat out of line in terms of price with the underlying stock, but such a condition rarely lasts too long. As an example, consider the charts in Figure 6.4 comparing the cash market S&P 500 index with the S&P index shares (SPY).

∎ FIGURE 6.1 Opening Gaps in Amgen. Arrows show opening gaps down. Note how prices reversed direction following opening gaps as illustrated. See Figure 6.2 for prices reversing in the opposite direction. Note that not all opening gaps down return to trade within the previous day's range.

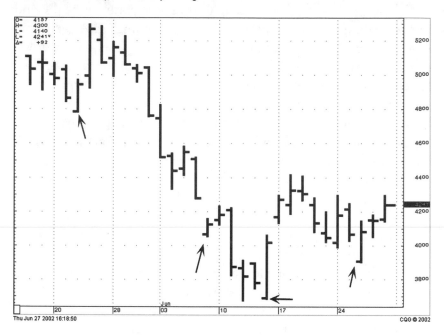

∎ Short-Term Considerations in Using Fundamental Analysis with SSFs

As indicated previously, fundamentals are often longer term in their effect on prices. Therefore, using fundamentals for day trading SSFs is not recommended. Instead, a technically oriented approach may be more effective given the need for immediate information and immediate response in short-term and day trading. This is not to say that those who follow fundamental market analysis cannot profit in SSFs, but I do believe, based on my experience and observations, that some of the inherent problems with fundamental analysis limit the efficacy of this approach in short-term and day trading.

■ FIGURE 6.2 Opening Gaps in Amgen. Note how prices reversed direction following opening gaps as illustrated. Arrows show opening gaps up and down.

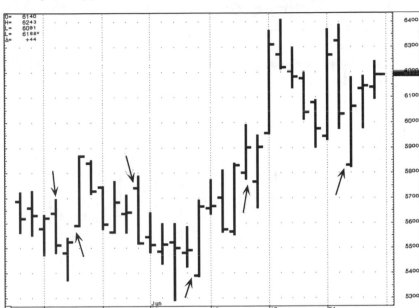

■ Available Alternatives

A number of possibilities are available as measures to resolve the problems and limitations in the use of fundamental analysis for short-term and day trading. These are as follows:

- *Technical analysis methods:* These are approaches to market forecasting and trading based on chart patterns, mathematical analyses, and other methods not involving or requiring knowledge of underlying fundamentals. The technical approach, as you will see in the next chapter, rejects the need for, and often the value of, fundamental factors in the decision-making process, trade selection process, and timing of trades.
- *Hybrid approach using technical and fundamental methods:* This approach is used by many traders with varying degrees of suc-

■ FIGURE 6.3 Opening Gaps in GE. Note how prices reversed direction following opening gaps as illustrated. Arrows show gap down openings. Note that not all opening gaps down result in profitable trades.

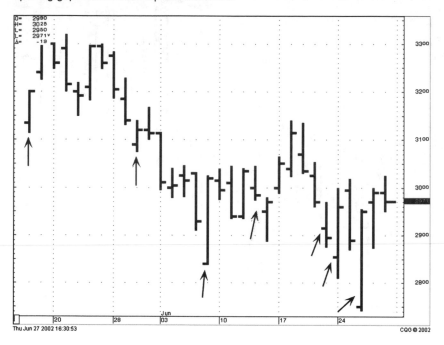

cess. It incorporates what traders believe to be the more significant and effective aspects of fundamentals and technicals and is also discussed in the next chapter.

- *Market structure analysis:* This area of market timing has grown considerably in popularity since the early 1990s. Several methods fall under this category, all of which depend, to varying degrees, on an understanding of who is buying and who is selling, who wants to buy or who wants to sell, and at what prices. In effect, these methods give traders information about the internal strength or weakness of a stock or futures market by examining the prices at which market makers are willing to buy or sell and in what quantities (i.e., the number of shares or contracts). The use of Nasdaq Level II data is the most popular market structure approach to short-term and day trading

■ FIGURE 6.4 The S&P cash index (top) versus the S&P stock index (SPY). Note the one-for-one correlation between trends in both of these markets.

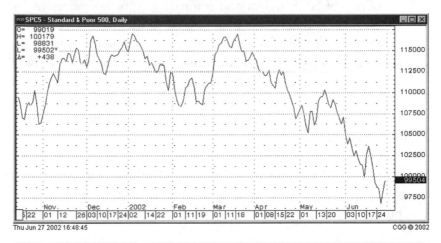

in stocks. The Market Profile™ work of J. Peter Steidlmayer is another example of this approach (Porcupine Press, 1986).

- *Potpourri:* This *method,* which may seem peculiar to you, is, in fact, the one that most traders use. I italicize the term *method* because, in effect, this is not really a trading approach at all. It is a hodgepodge of often loosely connected facts and opinions; technical and fundamental information; intuition; instinct; fantasies; emotions; news; broker and newsletter writer opinions; tips and advice gathered from friends, family, and/or Internet chat rooms; and even astrology. Although the vast majority of SSF traders and traditional futures traders use a potpourri approach, it is by no means either a testable procedure or a valid one. More often than not, those who follow no solid trading system or model are (and will be) ruled by emotions. Their trading will be neither systematic nor consistent. And unless these traders are exceptionally lucky or highly effective at risk management, in the long run their outcome will be negative.

Having looked at an introduction to fundamental analysis and its variations, let's now go to an overview of technical approaches in Chapter 7.

CHAPTER SEVEN

Technical Aspects

This chapter is especially important because many stock traders who have come to the SSF market have had training and experience in fundamental analysis only. I reiterate my view that fundamental analysis can be highly effective in determining intermediate and long-term trends, but it has its limitations when used for short-term and day trading. It has been my experience that the typical stock investor is severely deficient in the area of technical analysis, charting methods, trend determination, and market timing. The prevailing opinion that none of these skills are especially important for the investor is not valid. Stock market behavior throughout the world has become highly volatile since the mid-1980s. We live in troubled times, and violence is a way of life in several key areas of the world. Threats and acts of terrorism are daily events, and economic stability in many countries is threatened by effete or dysfunctional political systems. Uncertainty and volatility are rampant not only in futures but in stocks, currency relationships, and government policies. Virtually every day brings new concerns and challenges.

Furthermore, investors and traders have been blessed with access to a plethora of information, virtually all of which is available instantly via the Internet, business television, fax, and telephone. Stocks rise and fall sharply in reaction to news. Has this been a blessing or a curse?

Investors and traders have been blessed with the ability to place orders electronically that are filled within seconds. Brokers compete for customers by offering faster execution of trades, more information about the markets, opinions, research, recommendations, and stock analyses—all available at no additional charge. Some brokerage houses offer ten commission-free trades to new clients. The emphasis on speed of order execution encourages traders to act and react quickly. It invites traders to trade actively and for small price moves. Is the ability to place orders electronically and receive lightning-fast order execution a blessing or a curse?

Finally, the commission structure for stocks has also ushered in a new era of price speculation and short-term trading. If you can buy 100 shares of stock for a $14 commission and 5,000 shares of stock for the same $14 commission, then why not be more aggressive? Why not trade in large positions if you have the margin money? Why not increase the base of operations if the commission costs for doing so are minimal? Why not decrease the cost of doing business, thereby increasing the bottom line? Have lower commissions been a blessing or a curse?

Clearly, to those who can use the information, make intelligent and disciplined use of low commissions, and effectively integrate the trading platforms offered by brokerage firms with their market methodologies, the recent and significant advances described above can be a godsend. Yet to the newcomer, to the undisciplined trader, or to the average investor, these advances have only created losses. And they will likely continue to do so because most newcomers to trading, whether in stocks, SSFs, or futures, won't be able to use the necessary tools. Why not? Because they lack discipline, education, and experience. In this respect the SSF market is no different from any other market. To trade SSFs profitably, you need knowledge, perseverance, discipline, and solid risk management.

Finally, the fact that SSF margin requirements are 20 percent of the full value of the 100-share contract won't work in favor of most traders. The perception of success will become an elusive reality;

lower margins create more volatility. Even though the leverage af-forded by low margins *can* work for you, it more often than not works against you. Trading SSFs or, for that matter, any futures mar-ket on margin is like driving an 800-horsepower race car. Without training, you can kill yourself; with training, you stand a chance at winning in a highly competitive field.

Based on my lengthy experience in both the equities and futures markets, I believe that the best approach is a purely technical one because it facilitates discipline. Some, however, disagree with me, so the rest of this book may not interest those of you firmly com-mitted to the fundamental side. However, if you give me a chance, I think I can show you a few technical methods that may well en-hance your results with fundamental analysis.

Remember that in both the long and the short run, timing is not nearly as important in stocks as it is in futures. When you're deal-ing with a 20 percent margin as opposed to a 50 percent or 100 per-cent margin, you have less room and time for error, which is why timing is of the essence, regardless of whether you know the funda-mentals. I am not discounting the importance of timing in long-term stock investing; I am merely emphasizing an inherent fact about the markets.

Because the goal of technical analysis is to pinpoint the timing of a market move or change in trend to an exact point, I believe that all traders would do well to understand and employ technical analy-sis. No, technical analysis isn't the Holy Grail, but it certainly has the ability to help you pinpoint market timing.

■ Technical Systems

With the exception of the complete novice in futures trading, vir-tually everyone is familiar with one or several aspects of technical analysis. Technical analysis in stocks and futures is loosely defined as a study of futures trading data and its derivatives with the goal of forecasting price and/or determining specific market timing. In plain old English, this means that the technical analyst studies such things as price, volume, open interest, and chart patterns along with their interrelations, permutations, and combinations. The goal of most technical analysis is not necessarily prediction; it is the determination of specific entry and exit levels and/or specific price objectives for each signal. But prediction is not a requirement. Entry and exit signals alone are quite sufficient.

The roots of technical analysis run deep in the history of futures trading, even if it is uncertain who the first individual or group to employ it might have been. I am certain, however, that traces of technical analysis can probably be found as far back as ancient civilizations. Because technical analysis prides itself on having a quasi-scientific basis, you can understand how the continued exponential growth of scientific methodology has spilled over into the area of technical analysis (as well as fundamental analysis). As a consequence, we've seen a proliferation of literally hundreds of systems, methods, techniques, and trading approaches based on technical concepts.

Technical analysis certainly has its place in the world of futures trading, but as you might have guessed, it has its limitations as well. It is my conclusion that technical analysis is more suitable for short-term trading than for long-term trading. Although certain technical methods may be applied to long-term charts, the intricacies of technical analysis do not lend themselves easily to such things as contract changes (i.e., length of contract life) in the futures market.

Specifically, long-term technical analysis must employ long-term data. And the only continuous long-term data available to futures analysts are cash market data. Futures data start and stop with contract expirations and contract inceptions. The variability of prices from one contract to another as a function of such things as carrying charges, storage charges, and interest rates creates a gap that must be filled either by creation of artificial data or by some other statistical manipulation that is not necessarily representative of true underlying conditions. Because of this, we've seen a number of different approaches to technical analysis on weekly and monthly charts, resulting in some disagreement among followers of the various techniques. Some of the criticisms of technical analysis include these:

- Pure technical analysis ignores all extraneous inputs such as news, fundamentals, weather, and the like. This is seen as a detriment by some, as these factors can and do significantly affect prices. The technical trader however, claims that these factors influence prices and that it is therefore only necessary to study actual price trends and patterns.
- Technical analysis is a form of tunnel vision because it accepts input from no other method or technique when employed in its ideal form. Hence, the purely technical trader may not be trading with all relevant information.
- Technical analysis is so widely used, particularly by computer-generated trading programs, that many systems act in unison, thereby affecting prices in a fashion that is not representative of the true price structures. Technical trading signals can become self-fulfilling prophecies.
- Technical analysis cannot allow for good forecasting or determination of price objectives because it does not account for underlying economic conditions. In so doing, the trader is afflicted with tunnel vision.
- Technical analysis is not a valid scientific approach because most methods study prices based on price-related data. In a sense, one is attempting to predict the outcome of a dependent variable based on the history of the same dependent variable. If the variable is indeed dependent on circumstances external to it, then it is a fallacy to attempt such predictions without knowing the external circumstances.
- Technical analysis is a self-fulfilling prophecy and clearly typifies the greater fool theory. The "greater fool theory" is the belief that if you buy a particular stock, commodity, or piece of property, you need only wait for someone else who is a greater fool to sell it to. In the end, it is the individual stuck with the hot potato who pays the price of being the greatest fool.

These, then, are some of the objections to technical analysis. On the positive side, however, technical analysis attains its strength from the fact that it is a form of disciplined and essentially mechanical application of trading rules. In its ideal form, technical analysis leaves little or no room for interpretations of trading signals. In this way, it permits discipline to regulate trading. Naturally, these are ideal concepts and their application is most certainly dependent on the individual. Some advantages of the purely technical approach are these:

- Objectivity: The technical approach, in ideal form, is objective and specific. It is akin to scientific methodology. Objectivity minimizes the possibility of trader error prompted by emotional decisions.
- Specificity: The technical approach looks for specific indications from the data and then acts upon them. Hence, there should be little or no room for interpretation in a purely technical method. Decisions are objective and therefore reflect a quasi-scientific methodology.
- Mechanical: Many technical analysts claim their approach is totally mechanical. In other words, no extraneous information goes into buying/selling decisions. The system makes all the judgments and the trader follows them mechanically (if the system is implemented in its ideal form).
- Testable and verifiable: All results and indicators can be tested and verified historically. This makes the approach more scientific and lends credence to its use and value.
- Consistency and reliability: The technical approach should yield similar results regardless of who is using the system, provided their rules are the same.
- Ease of implementation: By virtue of the above, technical systems are claimed to be easier to implement than are fundamentally based systems.
- Computer application: Recently, the advent of lower-priced personal computer systems has made technical systems even less difficult to test and employ. Most of the truly mechanical systems can be programmed into computers, which will generate all buy and sell signals accurately. Computers can be programmed to send the signals to a broker for execution.

Much can be said in favor of technical analysis. However, with the growing ability of computer systems to develop and implement complex econometric models, fundamentally based computer models will most likely have a more pronounced impact on futures trading, particularly on SSFs. The result could very well be a hybrid approach that yields better performance than each method alone. This, however, is not yet the case. Whether technical, fundamental, or technofundamental, the ultimate action taken by the speculator will determine the success or failure of any trading system in SSFs, regardless of how promising computer tests of the system may be. Ideal situations are subject to the limitations of the weakest link. The trader is that link.

■ What's Best for You

I've observed that individuals who adhere strictly to one approach or another can do well in their trading. However, individuals who constantly shift from one technical approach to another, from one fundamental approach to another, or from an essentially fundamental point of view to a technical point of view will probably not do well because they don't allow sufficient time for their trading approach to reach fruition. My advice is to find one system or method and to stay with it.

The answer to the question, What's best for you? is not a simple one. After years of analysis and study, I can tell you that virtually any systematic approach to futures trading can be successful, provided that it contains the following three essential elements:

1. Specific entry and exit indicators. By this I mean that rules for entering and exiting trades must be as specific and mechanical as possible. Interpretation about the validity of a given signal to buy or sell must be kept to an absolute minimum. There should also be reliability between different users of the method. In other words, two individuals using the same approach in the same market at different locations and without collaboration should ideally reach the same conclusion. This is essential for success!

2. Risk management. For a system to be successful, it must have an automatic way to limit losses. There should be a maximum permissible dollar loss or a specific level beyond which losses should not go on, based on a systematic approach.
3. Flexibility. The system must be sufficiently flexible to trade both sides of the market, long and short. Furthermore, the system should do well in all types of markets, trending and trendless (though this is a lot to ask).

■ Success at the Extremes

Provided these three essential elements are present and provided the method of trade selection has even a slightly greater probability than chance, the end result should be profitable. Many systems are capable of generating trading signals that are profitable more than 50 percent of the time. Numerous approaches, both technical and fundamental, have shown even better performance by applying various trend filters and preselection criteria.

The technical approach to risk management can yield excellent results. The same is true of the fundamental approach. However, a middle of the road technical and fundamental system or a variety of different technical systems all applied at one time, or a variety of different fundamental techniques all applied at one time, is likely to produce poor results. Avoid mixing too many factors or systems into one process.

As you attempt to find answers best suited to your needs, consider the points I have raised in this chapter and make your decisions methodically after studying the available information. Finally, consider the possibility that a fully mechanical trading system may be your key to profitable trading. Successful traders are found at both ends of the continuum. Some traders are analytical. They enjoy the decision-making process, preferring to avoid purely mechanical approaches. Both avenues can yield profits in SSF trading.

The choice to follow fundamentals or technicals is a difficult one, but it is one that must be made on the basis of existing realities. Even though a great deal of negative comment has been made in recent years about the value of fundamentals, fundamentals are the ultimate factors that determine price. For the average speculator, however, the time, cost, and competition characteristic of involvement with large firms make fundamental analysis a difficult prospect. Technical trading approaches will work well provided they are applied in a thorough and disciplined fashion. They are less costly, less time consuming, and more adaptable to today's computer technology. Hence, they are the method of choice for most speculators.

CHAPTER EIGHT

Major Categories of Technical Indicators and Trading Methods

This chapter reviews how trend lines and moving averages are used in trading stocks and futures to reacquaint you with the methods and present the topic in an organized and concise fashion with objective rules of application.

Trading SSFs is more like trading futures than it is like trading stocks because the margin required to trade SSFs is considerably lower than the margin required to trade stocks. Therefore, the experienced futures trader who uses methods of technical analysis has an immediate advantage over the stock trader who has never traded futures; after all, the majority of traders in traditional futures are technically oriented. It's true that such fundamentals as weather, crop conditions, supply and demand, and government policies can impact the grain and soybean futures markets. But it's also true that technical traders can see signs of new market moves in stocks and traditional futures, often before they begin, because (at least theoretically) fundamentals influence trader action that in turn influences price that in turn causes technical indicators to change.

I suggest that if you plan on trading the SSF market successfully, you will be a very effective fundamental analyst of the underlying stocks, as well as a student of economics and history, or you will be an effective technical analyst.

To assist those who wish to expand their technical analysis horizons to the methods that can be used with SSFs, I emphasize the following areas.

■ Traditional Chart Patterns

Even with the most limited amount of experience in technical analysis, you know that much of this approach depends on the analysis of graphs and charts depicting the price history of a market, an approach popularized by Robert D. Edwards and John Magee in 1948. In spite of its relative subjectivity, many traders use this approach in selecting trades and projecting trends in the stock and futures markets. Gramm and Dodd described a variety of price patterns, also known as chart formations, which purportedly have predictive value in allowing traders and investors to determine which stocks or futures markets to buy and sell.

Chart patterns remain the subject of many books on technical analysis in spite of the difficulty proving their true value statistically. Nonetheless, they are still used by many traders and investors. In essence, the effective use of these patterns depends as much on art and experience as it does on objectivity. Some traders can use them very effectively, whereas others are incapable of profiting from their use. This holds true for stocks as well as futures and will also likely hold true for SSFs. The simple fact: the profitability of a method is limited by the operator.

One of the most popular techniques of chart analysis is the use of trend lines, a method used for determining levels of support and resistance as well as buy and sell signals. Trend lines have been used by traders and investors for many years and have been studied by virtually every futures trader. This approach has merit as a method for trading SSFs, as long as you are aware of its limitations.

Trend lines appear to be effective, yet most traders are unfamiliar with a number of important aspects of trend line analysis. The problems begin with definitions. Because it's important to have a solid working definition of a trend line, let's take a look at the definition of *trend line analysis* to keep our methods and procedures as operational as possible. This, in turn, reduces inconsistency and with it a degree of error.

My definition of a trend line is a line connecting a minimum of three nonconsecutive turning points on a chart. Unfortunately, a definition of this nature is so general that it leaves too much room for interpretation (as well as misinterpretation). So let's expand the definition to include four essential types of trend lines with which you should be familiar:

1. Support line: A line connecting at least three nonconsecutive turning points on a bar chart, slanting in a horizontal or upward direction and running under prices on the bar chart. Figure 8.1 shows several typical support lines in a futures contract.
2. Resistance line: A resistance line consists of at least three nonconsecutive turning points running above the price on a bar chart and slanting downward or horizontally. Figure 8.2 illustrates several support and resistance lines in a futures contract. Figure 8.3 shows some resistance lines in a futures contract.

In addition to the two basic types of trend lines, there are two variations:

1. Support return line: The extension of a support line into the future after the trend line has been penetrated in order to determine possible future price resistance.
2. Resistance return line: The extension of a resistance line into the future once it has been penetrated by price in order to determine possible future support. Examples of support and resistance return lines are shown in Figures 8.4, 8.5, and 8.6. Note how prices often come back to their return lines after penetration.

■ FIGURE 8.1 Various Support Lines in a Futures Contract. Note how support lines are drawn under price lows. Note also how quickly prices tend to decline once a support line has been penetrated.

■ FIGURE 8.2 Various Support and Resistance Lines in a Futures Contract. Note how support and resistance lines, once penetrated, can serve as good indicators of a new trend. Note also that resistance lines are drawn above price highs.

▮ FIGURE 8.3 Resistance Lines in a Futures Contract

▮ FIGURE 8.4 Return Lines. Once a support line or resistance line has been penetrated, it can be extended to form a "return" line.

█ FIGURE 8.5 Return Lines. The portion of the trend lines that extends past the point of trend line penetration is called the "return" line.

█ FIGURE 8.6 How Return Lines Develop as Future Support and/or Resistance

■ Using Trend Lines in SSF Trading

Trend lines can be applied to the SSF market in a variety of ways, depending on the goal(s) of the trader and the time frame(s) in which trading is being carried out. Because SSFs are more volatile than stocks as a result of their lower margin requirements, they are more suitable for day trading. Although the application of trend lines to day trading (or short-term trading) is similar to that of position trading (i.e., trades lasting more than a few days and up to several months), the psychology of traders using trend lines is different.

Traditionally, trend lines were used as indicators for buying and selling at specific breakout points both up and down (as illustrated previously in this chapter). This traditional approach is based on the expectation that once a trend line has been penetrated in one direction or another, a significant price movement is likely to continue in the direction of the penetration. Therefore, a penetration above a resistance trend line is expected to yield a profitable buy trade, whereas a penetration of a support line is expected to yield a profitable short trade. Because no method, system, or timing indicator is 100 percent accurate, a profitable outcome of such signals is not certain. Nevertheless, trend lines do appear to have some degree of validity as points for buying and selling SSFs (and other markets as well).

Other Applications for Trend Lines in SSF Trading

Trend line analysis can be used in SSF trading in other ways. Some traders turn bearish on the market when its support line has been penetrated to the downside, but they won't sell short immediately. Instead, they'll wait until prices recover and sell on the rally. Alternatively, penetration of a resistance line is frequently taken to indicate a change in trend to the upside. Many traders use the resistance line's points to establish short positions when a market rallies. Both techniques are commonly known and widely followed. It is difficult to state which procedure is the most reliable, but both have validity in SSF trading. Illustrations of these applications are shown in Figures 8.7, 8.8, and 8.9.

FIGURE 8.7 Trend Lines and Signals with Retracement Following Breakouts Up

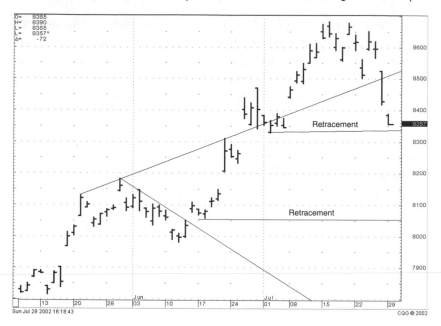

FIGURE 8.8 Trend Lines and Signals: Using Retracements. The breakout at B is followed by a retracement at A, and a retracement to C after another breakout at D.

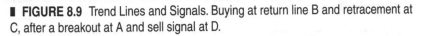

FIGURE 8.9 Trend Lines and Signals. Buying at return line B and retracement at C, after a breakout at A and sell signal at D.

Use of Trend Lines in Intraday SSF Trading

Trend line analysis can also be effective for intraday SSF trends. Ideally, a one-hour, half-hour, or ten-minute price chart of active SSF markets is best for this purpose. Support, resistance, and trend line returns can be implemented on an intraday time frame using these charts. Illustrations of these techniques on intraday price charts are shown in Figures 8.10, 8.11, and 8.12. Figures 8.13 and 8.14 show trend line analysis on a one-minute and five-minute open/high/low/close price chart for those of you considering using trend line analysis on SSFs in extremely short-term time frames.

■ Suggestions for Applying Trend Line Analysis

Many traders now prefer more sophisticated computer-generated signals over traditional trend line analysis. They have abandoned trend line methods in favor of these more complex and compli-

▌FIGURE 8.10 Trend Line Signals on Intraday Data

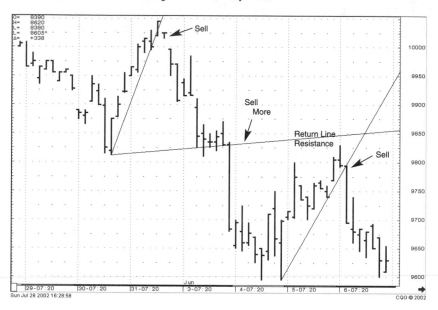

▌FIGURE 8.11 Trend Line Signals on Intraday Data

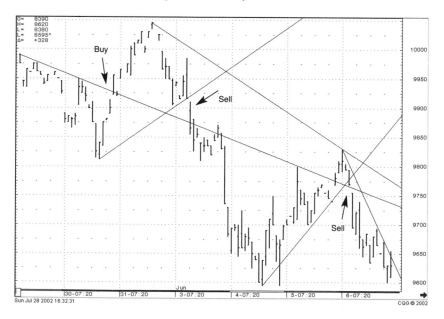

▌ FIGURE 8.12 Trend Line Signals on Intraday Data

▌ FIGURE 8.13 Trend Line Signals on Five-Minute Chart

■ **FIGURE 8.14** Trend Line Signals on One-Minute Chart

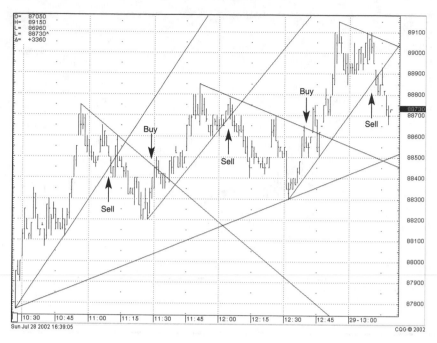

cated, but not necessarily more effective, systems. (Some of the more intricate approaches will be discussed in later chapters.) Based on my experience and observations, the trend line technique of buying on reactions to trend line support during an uptrend and selling on rallies to trend line resistance during a downtrend can be a very effective technique in both stock and futures trading. And it should also be a reliable method for SSF trading.

The main focus in trend line analysis should be on an accurate determination of signals as well as on a consistent application of signals. Trend line followers have a tendency to adapt trend lines to fit their particular needs or market bias. But this temptation must be strictly avoided. You should attempt to adhere as strictly as possible to trend line rules if success is to follow. Here are some suggestions how you might implement the trend line technique:

- The single most important rule: Trade with the trend. This is the most frequently stated but most commonly misunderstood and overlooked aspect of successful speculation. Determining the major trend is not an especially difficult task, even for the novice SSF trader. Professional traders should find this step simple to implement consistently.
- Assuming you have determined the major trend of prices and assuming that the trend is up, the next step would be to draw support lines under the market.
- Extend the trend lines into the future.
- Determine the intersection point of trend line and price for the next market period (i.e., day, hour, etc.) Enter your price order slightly above the support line. I suggest a little leeway in order entry as many other traders will probably be entering their orders at or about the trend line price.
- A good rule regarding stop losses: Liquidate your position as soon as your price has closed below the trend line, thereby negating its value as support and generating a reversing signal. Those willing to take a slightly greater risk can wait for two consecutive closings below the trend line, provided the first closing doesn't exceed the maximum permissible per-trade losses (if such a limit is being used).
- You can determine your objective in any of several ways. One technique is to reverse positions once a new trend line signal has formed. Another method is to sell your positions once a resistance line has been touched or approached. In the absence of a resistance line, other techniques could be used in liquidating a position, such as successively changing stops as the price continues to move in your favor (known as *a trailing stop*). The reverse procedure would hold true for selling short on the penetration of support.

All of my examples are drawn from real-time trading and represent real situations in the futures markets. I could have very carefully chosen many examples illustrating ideal or perfect situations, but because the perfect situation is the exception rather than the rule, I have given you as many current examples as possible.

■ Summary

Trend line analysis is a viable technique that seems to have experienced considerably less following in recent years as a result of the advent of more complex mathematical approaches requiring computer analysis. Nonetheless, the use of trend line analysis in SSFs is a viable methodology that is specific, simple, and cost effective. At least four different types of trend line signals, each adaptable to specific situations in stocks, futures, and SSFs, are:

1. Sell on support trend line penetration.
2. Buy on resistance line penetration.
3. Buy on drop to support return line.
4. Sell on rally to resistance return line.

Trend line analysis is likely to be a worthwhile technique in SSFs as it is not practiced by as many traders now as was the case in the past before computer applications were used (although these methods may not necessarily be as effective). Trend line analysis can provide exit and entry points based on support and resistance within existing trends in SSFs. And it is reasonably objective and can be applied in a fairly consistent fashion, provided simple objective rules are followed consistently.

Trend line trading does not require complex interpretations or sophisticated equipment. It is therefore ideal for the newcomer, although it can also be used by professional traders as long as the rules for its application are followed consistently. And, finally, trend line trading can be used on daily or intraday data.

■ Moving Averages

A more objective method of technical analysis (as opposed to trend lines) uses moving averages (sometimes referred to as MAs). Popularized by Richard Donchian in the 1950s, the use of moving average–based methods for market timing has its strengths and liabilities. Donchian advanced the idea that a more responsive type of trend line could be used to establish buy and sell signals as well as support and resistance. Rather than the familiar (straight-line) method described earlier, Donchian theorized that a moving average of prices could be used as a market-timing indicator.

A *moving average*, or MA, is a simple mathematical calculation of prices that provides up-to-date, or moving, indications of market activity. Instead of examining price highs and lows for the entire history of the current contract, a moving average constantly moves forward in time, examining only a defined segment of time or number of prices, particularly in the recent past.

A 10-day moving average, for example, uses prices for the last 10 days, ignoring what has transpired before. In so doing, it provides a more sensitive measure by taking an average of the last 10 days' prices and on the 11th day dropping the oldest day in the data and recalculating the average with the current daily data. At any given point, only 10 days of data are used—the most recent 10 days.

Theoretically, price movement above the moving average is considered bullish. If a market has been in an uptrend but then falls below the moving average line, this is taken to indicate a probable change in trend from bullish to bearish. Conversely, if the market has been declining (i.e., it is below its moving average) and then crosses above its moving average, a bullish signal seems indicated.

Although relatively simple to understand and straightforward in its construction and interpretation, the moving average has undergone many changes both in construction and application during the last 40 years. In only a few cases have the changes and additional efforts been fruitful.

Figures 8.15 through 8.19 show several markets plotted with moving averages of different lengths in the futures markets. The simple rules are as follows:

- When prices close *above* the MA, a buy signal occurs.
- When prices close *below* the MA, a sell signal occurs.

Although the selection of one moving average as a means of timing entry and exit is certainly a technique that appears to have potential, some have found that two moving averages, and perhaps

▮ FIGURE 8.15 Moving Average Buy Signals

▮ FIGURE 8.16 Moving Average Sell Signal

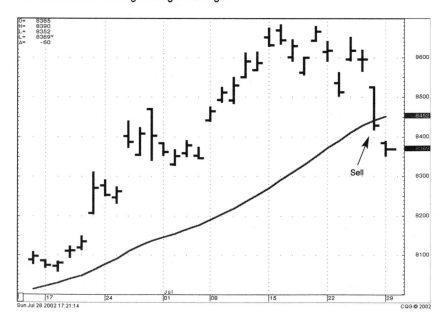

▌ FIGURE 8.17 Moving Average Buy and Sell Signals

▌ FIGURE 8.18 Moving Average Buy and Sell Signals

three, tend to serve the purpose better. Whereas one moving average will indicate the trend only over a specific length of time, the addition of one or two moving average indicators could significantly improve results by providing several measures of market strength or weakness.

Theoretically, buy signals are generated when two moving average lines cross in the upward direction, and sell signals are generated when two moving averages cross in the downward direction (see Figures 8.19 and 8.20). Finally, a third moving average could be added to further verify timing or to provide more evidence of a change in trend.

The application of various moving averages to determine buy and sell indications has received considerable study over the years. Certain combinations in certain markets are optimal, whereas other combinations appear not to be particularly fruitful. Specifically, the 4-day, 9-day, and 18-day moving averages seem to work best together in the futures markets.

Money managers and speculators frequently use moving average signals, whose popularity derives from their meeting many specific criteria of effective systems. These criteria are the following:

- Moving average signals are specific and objective.
- Moving average signals can keep you in the market at all times—closing out a long, going short, and covering a short when going long. This is valuable because you will have a position when major moves begin.
- Moving averages are trend-following systems. In other words, when a good trend is set in motion, the likelihood of the moving average's having a position consistent with the trend is very high.

Whatever combination of moving averages you may be using, the fact remains that they are mechanical and easily implemented. Unfortunately, they don't do well in certain types of markets. These are primarily sideways or choppy markets, in which prices move back and forth in a small or large range, but over such a brief period of time that the moving average indicators are almost constantly

■ FIGURE 8.19 Moving Average Lines Crossing to Generate Buy and Sell Signals

■ FIGURE 8.20 Moving Average Lines Crossing to Generate Buy and Sell Signals

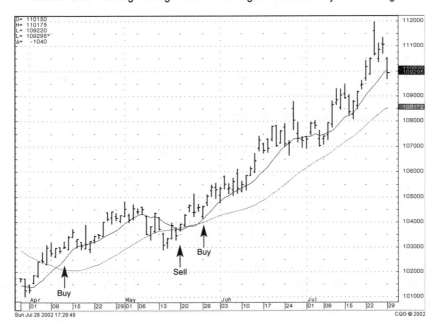

out of phase with market activity. The result is low accuracy and numerous losses.

Because the SSF market functions more like a futures market than a stock market, the odds are that, due to increased volatility, moving average systems used in a traditional approach could result in more false signals than they do in the underlying stocks for SSFs. Only time will tell if traditional moving average methods can be used effectively in the SSF market. I do believe, however, that the use of fundamentals to preselect a market trend or expectation, when combined with moving averages used for timing, can be a winning marriage.

In a choppy or trendless market, moving average–based systems may not fare well and, indeed, may result in worse performances than those of other technical systems. However, in a trending market, moving average systems shine. There are various solutions to this problem. They are discussed in Chapters 9 and 11.

Reviewing Moving Average Signals

To use a three moving average method for trading SSFs, do the following:

- Compute the three moving average lengths.
- Buy when all three moving averages have crossed in an upward direction. (If using one moving average, then buy when the price closes above the moving average.)
- Sell and sell short when all three moving averages have crossed in a downward direction. (If using one moving average, then sell when the price closes below the moving average.)
- Moving average systems are based on reversals. In other words, when a long position is closed out, a short position is entered. When a short position is closed out, a long position is entered.

Moving average systems can be valuable to the new trader. Though they may result in larger-than-acceptable risk, they do assist with self-discipline and risk management. Before you consider using moving averages for trading, study this approach very thoroughly because it has its limitations as noted below. There are many variations on the moving average theme. I suggest you familiarize yourself with these before going forward.

Limitations of Moving Averages

There are two significant limitations to the use of moving averages. They are:

1. Disappointing accuracy results in large drawdowns. This means your account equity can drop significantly as the result of a string of losing trades. By the time the system turns higher, you will be out of capital.
2. Moving average systems are often reversing systems; that is, they require you to reverse your position from short to long and vice versa. This means you don't know your stop loss before entering a trade, which limits your ability to determine your risk before you trade. And this is not a good idea, particularly for the new trader.

■ Summary

Following a discussion of the general aspects of moving averages, certain specifics of moving average techniques were reviewed and illustrated. Strengths and weaknesses of traditional moving average systems were reviewed. The use of moving average–based systems in SSF trading is worth considering despite their limitations, the most significant of which is unsatisfactory accuracy. By using variations on the theme of moving averages, results can be improved considerably.

The moving average systems available today are much more sophisticated and well tested than they have been in the past. Consistent application of moving average techniques has validity as a successful methodology for technical traders. The use of such techniques should not be discounted by traders inasmuch as they are specific, mechanical, trend following, and relatively simple to implement. Though there can be large drawdowns and periods of persistent losses in zigzag-type ("whipsaw") markets, the potential of moving average systems in trending markets is tremendous. Additional applications of moving-average-based systems can be found in my book *Profit in the Futures Markets* (Bloomberg, 2002).

CHAPTER NINE

Spread Trading in Single Stock Futures

Perhaps the most interesting, and potentially profitable, tool in futures trading is the *spread*. Yet in spite of its potential and validity as a trading method, it is not understood by most traders and therefore not generally employed by the trading public. On the other hand, professional traders in the futures and options markets use spreads frequently as vehicles to profitable trading. Why is it that spreads are so poorly understood by the public? The answer here, as in most cases, is a combination of ignorance and fear. One reason for this problem is that a spread involves two opposite positions in the same market or in related markets at the same time. This can be confusing, especially to the new trader.

It seems paradoxical that with the wealth of information available today about trading systems and methods, there should exist such a weak spot in market knowledge. I suggest that even futures traders who are familiar with the use of spreads not skip this chapter, as I offer some important points about the use of spreads in SSFs—points that may serve you well in the short as well as the long run.

■ What Is a Spread and How Does It Work?

A spread is precisely what its name implies: it involves the purchase of one contract and sale of another contract in different months or in the same or different futures markets, most often simultaneously, in order to profit from the differential strength or weakness between the two contracts or the two different markets. Putting it simply, when you enter a spread, you go long and short either in different contract months of the same market (or SSF) or in two different markets (or SSFs).

As noted earlier, when you enter a spread, you buy and sell at the same time; however, you do so in different contract months of the same market or SSF or in the same contract month of two different but related markets or SSFs. By being long and short at the same time, you try to take advantage of the fact that, at times, different contract months of the same SSF or market, or the same contract month of different markets or SSFs, rise and fall at different rates of speed or by different amounts.

If this sounds a bit intricate or confusing, consider the fact that conditions affecting the price of June General Motors futures may be considerably different than conditions and factors that may affect the December General Motors futures contract. How so? It's really very simple. Assume that it is now April. Assume also that General Motors (GM) shows strong car sales at the present time with the odds of strong car sales continuing for several months. However, projections looking ahead to December are not nearly as optimistic. In other words, GM expects car sales to be lower in December than they are now.

What will happen to the price of General Motors futures? Investors will want to buy the June futures contract, expecting that the stock and the futures will rise in response to the good news. Yet, they may not want to buy the December futures, because they believe, based on the report, that the stock may not be as strong later in the year. What happens? The June futures contract rises faster than the December, or the June futures contract rises while the December contract either remains the same or declines.

An investor who bought June futures would make money as they rise in price. An investor who bought December futures might make no money or could lose money. An investor who bought June futures and sold short December futures could make money on both ends of this strategy. However, in this case, the investor who bought June and sold short December might make money *even in a declining market!* How so? Think about it: if the price of General Motors declines, then the June contract may decline only by a small amount, while the December contract may decline by a larger amount. The investor has lost money on the long position, but he has made more money on the short December position than he has lost on the long June position.

As you can see, there are a number of possible outcomes with a spread. They are as follows:

Spread Behavior	*Outcome*
Long position goes up more than short position	You make money
Long position goes up while short position goes down	You make money
Long position goes down while short position goes down more than long	You make money
Long position goes down more than short position	You lose money
Long position goes up less than short position	You lose money
Long goes down while short goes up	You lose money
Long and short move the exact same amount	You lose commission

In other words, a spread can give you possibilities that a "flat position" (i.e., long or short but not spread) can. That's the good news. The bad news is that unless you use the right method(s) of selecting spreads, they will not work for you. Whether your methodology is based on fundamentals or technical or a combination of both, you still have to use effective risk management as well as a proven selection approach.

The two basic categories of spreads are intramarket spreads, or spreads in different contract months of the *same* market, and intermarket spreads, or spreads using similar contract months in two different markets.

Volatility

While some spreads are less risky than flat positions in SSFs, some spreads are much more risky than flat positions. The degree of risk in a spread depends essentially on two factors:

1. The difference in time span between the contract months in an intramarket spread determines one aspect of spread volatility. The larger the time span between the two months being spread, the larger the volatility, the larger the risk, and the larger the possible profit. A long March Ford versus a short June Ford spread is not as inherently volatile as a long March Ford versus a short December Ford spread.
2. The degree of similarity between two different SSFs is also an operative factor in the volatility of an SSF spread. A spread between June General Motors and June Ford will likely not be as volatile as a spread between June General Motors and June Chevron-Texaco.

Finally, the SSF market also allows spreading between SSFs and narrow-based indexes (NBIs) as well as spreads within NBIs. As an example, consider the following possible spreads:

- Long Ford versus short the Oil Services NBI
- Long Wal-Mart versus short the Drugs NBI
- Long the Defense NBI versus short the Investment Banking NBI

As you can appreciate, there are literally hundreds if not thousands of possibilities. A good rule of thumb in trading SSF spreads is to have a fundamental basis for trading the spread. In other words, I suggest that you begin with an idea that makes sense. This will become clear to you as we examine a few spread examples in the pages that follow.

Here are a few spread examples:

Long June AT&T futures/short December AT&T futures
Long June Ford futures/short June General Motors futures

Both of the above trades are spreads. The first spread, long June AT&T futures/short December AT&T futures is an intramarket spread because it involves two different contract months in the same stock. The second spread, long June Ford futures/short June General Motors futures is an intermarket spread because it involves two different stocks.

But why trade spreads? The simple and initial explanation is that conditions in stocks change over time. What may be bullish in the short term may be bearish in the long term. The bull trends of today become the bear trends of tomorrow. The prospects for AT&T over the next six months may be very positive, but nine months or a year from now conditions may not be as promising. Could it be possible to take advantage of such natural fluctuations in market trends and underlying conditions for a stock? Yes, indeed it can. The spread allows you to do so. A more specific explanation of how follows.

Consider the long June Ford futures/short June General Motors futures spread. How can this spread work to make money for you? Consider the possibility that over the next three months the profit picture at Ford is likely to improve dramatically at the same time conditions at General Motors will deteriorate as a function of various fundamental factors. In this case, would it be possible to buy Ford and sell short General Motors, making money on both ends of the game?

Could Ford increase its share price at the same time General Motors shares decline? Yes, indeed, this is possible, and, moreover, it happens all the time. Stocks move in their own directions even within the same industry group. One airline can do well while another can falter. One semiconductor chip maker can make huge profits while another makes only small profits. Can one group of stocks rise while another falls or rises less quickly? Can one stock fall sharply while another declines only slightly? Yes! These are some of the conditions that create spread opportunities.

Buy the Airlines—Sell the Petroleum Stocks

As a further example of a spread in SSFs, consider the following fundamental scenario: The economy has been strong. Airline passenger traffic is at a ten-year high. The economic forecast calls for even more travel. The earnings outlook for the next year is very positive. A number of industry analyses are forecasting a price rally in most of the major airlines. At the same time, the price of petroleum appears to be reaching a peak. Forecasts of petroleum production suggest that prices will decline over the next three to six months.

Is there a way you could take advantage of this situation? Here are some of the possibilities using SSFs:

- You could buy one or more of the airlines stocks.
- You could sell short one or more of the petroleum stocks.
- You could buy one or more airline SSF contracts.
- You could sell short one or more petroleum SSF contracts.
- You could buy an airline SSF index.
- You could sell short a petroleum index SSF.
- You could buy an airline SSF contract and sell short a petroleum SSF contract simultaneously.
- You could spread the airlines sector against the petroleum sector by using the SSF narrow-based indexes for these industry groups.
- You could buy an airline SSF contract while selling short a petroleum SSF contract.

As you can see, there are many choices. The most efficient of these, unless you consider yourself to be a long-term investor interested in dividends as well as profits on the price of the shares themselves, is to make your transaction in the SSF market where the margin required will be much lower than it would be in the underlying stocks themselves.

▌ Why Trade Spreads?

Trading in spreads allows you to capitalize on several possibilities at the same time. In some ways it gives you a greater degree of protection than trading in a "flat" position (by which I mean long or short but not specifically spread). If you trade intramarket spreads, then the degree of fluctuation between one contract month and another contract month of the same market will not be as large or as volatile as the degree of fluctuation between two different SSFs (i.e., intermarket spread). Hence, an intramarket spread can, at times, provide you more safety than a flat position or an intermarket spread. The lesser degree of volatility appeals to many traders, particularly those who have very limited funds with which to trade. The problem is, however, that very often such individuals are newcomers to the markets and have difficulty enough understanding how futures work, let alone how spreads work. The idea of being long and short in the same market at the same time is a source of confusion to many traders. Nonetheless, the spread can offer more stability if it is used correctly. As in virtually all cases of risk and reward, the less risk a trader takes, the less the potential reward.

Advantages and Disadvantages of Spread Trading

Spreading has its advantages and disadvantages. The advantages of spread trading in SSFs are as follows:

- Spread trading allows you to take advantage of divergent trends and/or differences in market strength either in the same SSF contract or in different SSFs at the same time.
- Margin requirements on an intramarket spread are often very low.
- Intramarket spreads tend to be less volatile and less risky (but this is not always the case).
- Intramarket SSF spread trading is a good way to speculate on the difference between current market trends and anticipated market trends.
- Professional traders often use spreads. Hence, you'll be in good company when you trade spreads (assuming that your trade selection is valid and you manage your risk effectively).

The disadvantages of spread trading in SSFs are these:

- It is difficult for many traders to understand spreads.

- Intermarket spreads in SSFs can be very risky and volatile. And at times they can be more volatile than flat positions in SSFs.
- You have to monitor the behavior of a spread itself as opposed to the behavior of each component of the spread, because spreads make or lose money on relative relationships and not as a function of each side (leg) of the spread in isolation.
- You must exercise caution in placing spread orders. All too often, spread traders exit and enter their spreads incorrectly by stating the buy or sell side erroneously.

How Spreads Can Make or Lose Money

Remember that spreads can make or lose money in a number of ways. Consider the following possibilities and their outcome.

Your position: You are long General Motors (GM) futures at $33 and short FORD (F) futures at $25. The spread between the two when you entered was $8 in favor of (stated as "premium to") GM. In other words, GM was priced $8 higher than F when you entered.

How you make or lose money on this spread: As long as the spread between GM and F increases (i.e., moves in the positive direction), you make money. Therefore, if the spread moves from $8, your entry price, to $12, you have made $4, or $400 in real money as you have 100 shares of the spread. If the spread becomes less positive by moving down from $8 to $3, you are losing money. In this case, you lost $5, or $500 in real money. Note, of course, that your loss is a paper loss (open loss) until you exit the spread.

Internal working of the spread: Continuing with the GM versus F example, note the following "internal" functioning of the spread and the outcomes.

1. Long GM $33, Short F $25: Spread = $8 on entry
   GM declines to $30. Your loss = $3
   F declines to $17. Your profit = $8
   You made $8 and lost $3: *Net gain* = $5

2. Long GM $33, Short F $25: Spread = $8 on entry
   GM goes up to $55. Your profit = $22
   F goes up to $30. Your loss = $5
   You made $22 and lost $5: *Net gain* = $17
3. Long GM $33, Short F $25: Spread = $8 on entry
   GM goes down to $30. Your loss = $3
   F goes up to $30. Your loss = $5
   You lost on both sides of the spread. *Net loss* = $8
4. Long GM $33, Short F $25: Spread = $8 on entry
   GM goes up to $40. Your profit = $7
   F goes down to $20. Your profit = $5
   You made money on both sides of the spread: *Net gain* = $12

(Of course, the above hypothetical examples assume exits as shown and don't include commissions or fees.)

Now consider a real-life situation in GM and Ford. Figure 9.1 shows a spread chart of GM versus F. This spread has made eight large moves since 1999. What do I mean by a "large move"?

Consider the following:

From point 1 to point A, the spread traversed a range of $32 to $62, or about $3,000 on the spread.
From point A to point B the spread dropped (i.e., GM losing to F) about $3,200 in value.
From point B to point C the spread gained about $22.
From C to D the spread lost about $25.
From D to E the spread gained about $17.
From E to F the spread lost about $17.
From F to G the spread gained about $30.
From G to H the spread lost about $16.

As you can see, the moves have been rather large as well as plentiful. As stated earlier, intermarket spreads such as this one are considerably more volatile than intramarket spreads. Furthermore, the automobile business from 1999 through 2002 has been highly volatile as well as sensitive to underlying economic conditions (as is usually the case). And this has helped create a highly volatile situation in the spread.

▌ FIGURE 9.1 The GM versus F Spread

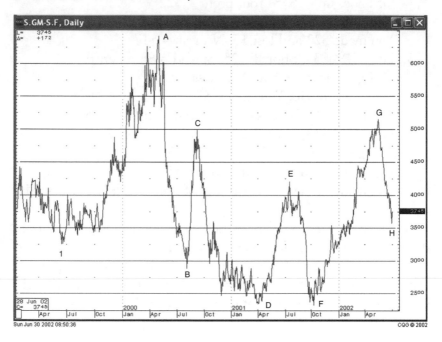

The spread shown in Figure 9.2—United Airlines (UAL) and American Airlines (AMR)—has also been subject to the trials and tribulations of the airline industry. As the chart shows, UAL lost considerable ground to AMR until February 2002, when the spread reversed and UAL gained back about $8 per share on AMR.

Finally, consider the Exxon Mobil (XOM) versus the UAL spread. Here we're comparing the performance of a petroleum stock with the performance of a major petroleum consumer, United Airlines. As you can see from Figure 9.3, XOM has gained steadily on UAL since 1999. In fact, the overall gain has been a whopping $73 per share (approximately). As you can see from the foregoing examples, the moves in intermarket spreads can be large and dramatic.

■ FIGURE 9.2 The UAL versus AMR Spread

■ FIGURE 9.3 The XOM versus UAL Spread

Spreads Based on Economic Trends

Spread timing can be based on economic fundamentals as well as on technical indicators (to be discussed next). As an example of economic conditions that might affect a spread, consider the following scenarios and actions in SSF spreads that might have good profit potential:

- You have reason to believe that the overall economy will improve over the next six months. You can buy the nearby month of GM (or other economy-sensitive stocks) and sell a distant month of GM stock. If the stock moves higher, then the front month will gain faster than the back month (e.g., March versus December).
- You have reason to believe that the major stock market averages will turn bearish. You can sell short the front month of an SSF and buy the back month of an SSF.
- You have reason to believe that major stock market averages will turn bearish. You can buy a precious metals SSF and sell an industrial stock SSF (e.g., GM). As an example of this spread see Figure 9.4. The chart shows Newmont Mining (NEM) versus Ford (F) as a spread. Note the large gain in NEM over F during the period from April 2001 to June 2002 as the U.S. economy contracted and stocks worldwide were on the decline.

▮ Technical Spread Indicators

Many technical indicators can be used in timing spread entries and exits. The more traditional methods, such as trendlines and moving averages, have distinct limitations (as explained in Chapter 8). One of the more effective indicators to use in futures trading, including SSFs, is the momentum indicator, or MOM, (i.e., the rate of acceleration of a price) and my adaptation of it, the momentum moving average (MOM/MA). If you are interested in the construction of the momentum moving average, I suggest consulting any of the leading books on technical analysis. Note also that most trad-

■ FIGURE 9.4 Newmont Mining versus Ford

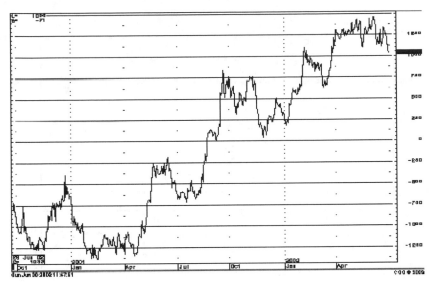

ing software programs have the MOM as one of their featured indicators. The rate of change (ROC) is essentially similar to the MOM and can also be used for spread timing as explained in this chapter.

The chart in Figure 9.5 shows the spread price at the top and the 28-day momentum indicator at the bottom. I have also shown two dashed lines that represent the entry, exit, and reversal points for the spread. The top dashed line is the point near which to exit the spread and/or reverse it while the bottom dashed line is the point near which to exit the spread and reverse in the other direction. This is a very simple application of spread timing. As you can see, the upper and lower dashed lines did a very good job picking reversal points for the spread at A through I. Clearly, the approach is not perfect, but it does offer considerable potential for timing spreads in SSFs.

Another approach to spread timing is to combine the MOM with its moving average. This method, which I call the MOM/MA, can pinpoint timing turns more accurately and isn't dependent on the upper and lower boundaries of the spread as sell and buy points. Figure 9.6 shows the Biogen (BGEN) versus IDEC Pharmaceuticals (IDPH) spread with momentum moving average timing.

▮ FIGURE 9.5 The GM versus F Spread with a 28-Period Momentum

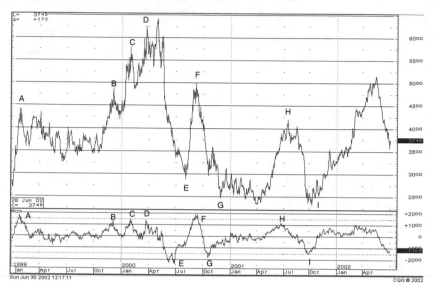

▮ FIGURE 9.6 Biogen (BGEN) versus IDEC Pharmaceuticals (IDPH)

I have not provided an exhaustive review of timing indicators that may be used with spreads. My goal in this chapter has been to familiarize you with spreads in SSFs along with showing that they can be highly profitable, with lower or higher risk depending on whether they are intramarket or intermarket spreads. I've also wanted to emphasize that you can use technical timing and/or fundamentals to take advantage of SSF spreading opportunities. For more information on the indicators discussed in this chapter, I refer you to my books, *The Compleat Day Trader* (McGraw-Hill, 1995), *The Compleat Day Trader II* (McGraw-Hill, 1998), and *Momentum Stock Selection* (McGraw-Hill, 2000).

CHAPTER TEN

Effective Order Placement

■ The Importance of Correct Order Placement

Perhaps the weakest link in the trading chain is the use of orders. Albeit a rather boring topic, order placement is nevertheless a very important aspect of trading and investing. It is especially important in short-term trading where every penny counts. Using the wrong order can cost you, whereas using the correct order can save you money.

There are three aspects of effective order placement that, if correctly carried out, will minimize your chances of error and maximize your potential for success. These factors are as follows:

- Knowledge of the types of orders that can be used and when to use them
- Organization and follow-through in order placement
- Knowing when to avoid certain orders as a function of market conditions and the given futures exchange

Let's examine these issues more thoroughly.

■ Types of Orders

Although there are relatively few types of orders, their correct and timely use is critically important. All too often traders misunderstand the meaning of certain order types and, on receiving a bad price execution of their trade(s), either attempt to blame their broker or find fault with the electronic network through which they placed their online order. A thorough knowledge of order placement can prevent errors and considerable frustration, as well as poor price fills (which cost you money). Since the advent of electronic order entry, it is even more important to understand and use orders correctly.

Once an order has been placed electronically and confirmed, it is irrevocable. The result of the order is your responsibility; consequently, if you place an incorrect order electronically, the liability is yours alone. Since the late 1990s, when electronic order entry became widely used in many markets, I've seen traders commit serious and costly blunders, particularly in thinly traded markets or at times of the day when markets are not actively traded. To avoid becoming a victim, whether you are a professional or part-time trader, it is in your best interest to know what orders to use and when to use them. Even though the SSF market is an electronic market that offers transparent order execution (i.e., you know which market maker fills your order as well as the bids and offers), *this fact alone doesn't guarantee a good price execution if you make a mistake.*

In order to better understand orders, let's follow an order from its inception to its culmination. Let's assume you call your broker and place an order to buy one contract of General Motors futures "at the market." Specifically, this means you are willing to buy at whatever price can be obtained for you when your order reaches the market maker. You can place your order either online electronically or through a broker who will place the order for you. Adding the broker to the equation increases the amount of time it takes to fill your order as well as the commission costs.

If you call the order in to a broker, you now have two choices. Depending on the type of trading you do and the type of broker you have, you either hang up the phone or you hold on for your price fill. When your broker receives the order, she writes an order ticket containing your account number and specific order. The ticket is then time stamped, and the broker enters your order on her electronic order entry terminal and then waits for a price execution. More often than not, your SSF order will be filled and reported back to you in less than one minute, assuming that the SSF you picked is reasonably liquid (i.e., has sufficient trading volume). If, on the other hand, you place your order online, bypassing the physical broker, your order, assuming good liquidity and trading volume, could be filled and reported back to you in a matter of seconds.

The OneChicago market has structured the SSF exchange so as to give fair and equitable price execution through its system of market makers. This means that your order will, theoretically, be filled at a price that is reasonable within the constraints of the bids and offers for the given SSF. Nonetheless, market orders, even when entered electronically, still have their assets and liabilities (as do all order types).

■ The Assets and Liabilities of Market Orders

A market order is an order to buy or sell at the prevailing price, regardless of what that price may be. The good news is that your at-the-market order gets filled; the bad news is that you may not be pleased with the price you get, as you wanted to buy or sell at the prevailing price. Given the liabilities of market orders, I recommend that you avoid such orders unless it is absolutely necessary for you to enter or exit a trade. As a result, at-the-market orders are best used for short-term and day traders who do not have the time to wait for a market to come to their buy or sell prices. The advantage of a market order is speed of execution, but this is also the disadvantage. As with all things in life, we pay for our impatience either physically or emotionally or both. Don't use an at-the-market order unless you must.

Finally, don't use a market order in SSFs that trade a very small number of contracts. The reason you want to avoid market orders in such cases is that the bids and offers for the SSF could be far removed from each other. *If you place an order to buy or sell at the market, the odds are you may be filled at the high bid when buying and at the low offer when selling.*

Other types of orders—such as those above the market, below the market, or conditional orders—are executed in essentially the same way. Because they are resting orders, however, they are not filled immediately. Let's look at the different types of orders that are possible and the intricacies that may be involved with some of these orders.

■ Market-on-Close (MOC) Orders

A market-on-close (MOC) order is an instruction to the market maker to execute an order—to buy or to sell—at or near the close of trading. Your order is frequently executed during the last few seconds of trading and, in most cases, your price fill will not be too different from the closing price. Very frequently, such orders are filled in the closing price range.

On occasion, MOC orders don't result in particularly good fills. My experience indicates that these orders in most active markets don't result in terribly bad price fills, but a difference of several ticks between what you expected and what you received can occur. Before using this type of order, make certain it is a valid order type. As the SSF markets become more actively traded and the electronic order system overcomes its limitations, various types of orders may be accepted, although initially they may not be permitted.

On occasion, MOC orders work to your advantage, particularly when a market is very strong or very weak as the final minutes of trading approach. Assume, for example, that you would like to buy at the end of the day, and further assume that the market is weak. In such a case, the market will often drop even lower on the close, as those who were buying during the day place MOC orders to sell or sell at the market shortly before the close of the day session. If you are short and have a MOC order to buy, or if you want to go net long, chances are you will get a reasonably good fill, as many traders rush to sell out their long positions at or near the day's low.

The reverse often holds true with MOC orders to sell. If the market is sharply higher and you have a long position you would like to liquidate by the close or a short you would like to establish, this could be an ideal situation. Frequently, in a market that has been strong all day, we see a rush to the upside, bringing prices even higher at the end of the session. This happens because those who were short for the day place orders to cover their short positions prior to the close of trading. Massive buying then ensues, which runs prices up to your advantage, if you are on the correct side of the market. Because you will be selling, you may get a better price fill than you expected. Also, MOC orders should be avoided in thin markets, because they can result in poor price execution.

▌ Market-on-the-Open Orders

These are simple, self-explanatory orders entered before the opening to buy at the market as soon as the market opens. Typically, a great deal of activity characterizes market opens, but in thin markets this activity could result in a reasonably bad price fill. Some market analysts and advisors have strong sentiments against buying on the open, thinking the opening is not necessarily a good reflection of market activity. Indeed, on many occasions in the past, traders have witnessed significant reversals after a strong opening in a given direction.

Certainly, if our order was on the buy side on a sharply higher opening during one of the reversal-type days, then we would indeed be in jeopardy or vice versa during a sharply lower opening (see Chapter 11). If you trade through a broker as opposed to electronically, then you must specify to your broker what you want to do. The broker then executes the order for you on the opening. To place such an order electronically, all you need to do is enter an order at the market immediately on the opening of the day session trading. Remember to make sure that such orders are accepted by the exchange.

∎ Stop Orders

Stop orders are orders that are either above or below the market. They are described in the following sections.

Buy Stop

This is an order to buy at a given price above the market. When the indicated price is hit, your order becomes a market order and is filled at the best price possible thereafter. Such orders are used to exit a short position or enter a long position on market strength.

Sell Stop

A sell stop order is an order to sell at a price below the market. Once the order price is touched, your order becomes a market order. Such orders are used to exit a long position or enter a short position on market weakness. When used to exit an existing position, the term *stop loss* is used (see below).

Stop Loss

The term *stop loss* is applied to a position that offsets an existing position. As such, this order is no different than either a sell stop or a buy stop as described above. A stop loss order is designed to limit loss, hence its name. Orders are not entered as stop loss orders but rather in the variety of ways described earlier or in the sections that follow. Hence, *stop loss* is a generic term that could be applied to orders above or below the market.

Stop Limit

The stop limit order is a specific type of stop order used either above or below the market. A sell stop limit means that you want to sell below the market but at a price no lower than the price of your limit. In other words, you must be filled at your price or not at all. This is a good way to guarantee a fill at a certain price, but if the market goes through your price and doesn't trade at it, or the order can't be filled even at the limit price, your order won't be filled. You may not get the protection you want if you are using a stop limit as a stop loss. The reverse holds true for stop limit orders above the market.

Stop limits should be used when you want to avoid a bad fill, or when you are working with a precise technical level. I do not recommend using stop limits for the purpose of stop losses. As noted earlier, these orders may not be acceptable at the given electronic exchange or network you are using. Please be certain to check in advance.

Stop Close Only

This is an instruction to sell or buy within the closing minute of trading. A sell stop close only order will be executed during the closing minute of trading. A buy stop close only will be executed at or above the given price during the last minute of trading. Many times the fill price will not be in agreement with the last tick or settlement price due to the time span during which a stop close only order can be filled.

Remember—before using this order, make certain it is a valid order type. While this type of order is not usually accepted for electronic order entry, your broker may be willing to execute such an order for you manually assuming you release the broker from liability.

Good-Till-Canceled (GTC) Orders (Open Orders)

A good-till-canceled order means just that: an order in the market until you cancel it. As a matter of procedure, some brokerage firms clear the books of open orders at the end of every day's trading unless these orders are reentered.

Most short-term traders don't find it necessary to use good-till-canceled orders. They can be used when you'll be out of touch with the market, but I strongly suggest you not trade when you are not in touch with the markets. Therefore, you won't need to use a good-till-canceled order.

■ When to Use Certain Orders and When to Avoid Them

It is important to use the correct order at the right time inasmuch as this significantly affects the price at which you buy or sell and, of course, also affects your bottom line. One thing to remember about order placement is that you must be specific and decisive. Here are a few important things to remember when placing orders:

- Use market orders for buying and selling if you're a day trader in the SSF market. If you wait too long to get filled, then you may miss your opportunity.
- If you trade ultrashort term (i.e., day trade or short-term trade), you can also use limit orders to buy at the best price possible and sell at the best price possible. This can be readily accomplished by keeping track of the bids and offers of the market makers for the SSFs you're trading. In such cases, you attempt to buy at the lowest offering price and sell at the highest bid price. Note, however, that commission costs are usually higher on limit orders, and you also run the risk of not being filled.
- To a great extent the orders you use are a function of the system or method you are using. This is discussed in detail in the following section.
- Make certain you cancel open orders once they are no longer needed or valid.
- Keep a record of all orders that have been entered, particularly if you are trading in more than one SSF at a time.
- If you trade SSF spreads, be especially careful to enter the sell and buy orders correctly. Remember that to exit a spread such as long Ford versus short GM, you sell Ford and buy GM.

Many errors are made by incorrectly reversing the buy and sell orders.

- Before you "press the button" on electronic entries of SSF orders, double-check and triple-check the quantity as well as the order type (and price) you have entered in the computer. Your trading platform (i.e., software) may help you by asking if you are certain that your order is correct.
- Avoid at-the-market orders in thinly traded SSFs.
- Keep current on the types of orders that are acceptable in the SSF markets because this may change over time. I suggest frequent visits to the OneChicago Web site at <www.onechicago .com> or ask your broker to keep you up-to-date.
- Have a backup method of order entry, particularly if you day trade SSFs. After all, if you enter orders electronically and your computer or your connection line fails, you'll need a backup method for entering your orders. Make certain that the firm you are trading with has a dial-up voice number you can use in an emergency.
- Don't make the mistake of believing that because you use an electronic order entry, you'll automatically get fair or reasonable price execution on your orders.
- If you replace an order or change an existing order, be certain you indicate any change when you place your order. Most electronic order-entry procedures allow such a procedure, but you must make certain that orders have been canceled where and when necessary before you replace them.

▌ Order Types as a Function of the System or Method Being Used

As noted earlier, the type of order you use is also a function of the system or method you are using to trade SSFs. Given the three basic categories of trading methods, the choices are often clear and concise. Here are some examples.

Systems That Buy or Sell at the Market

Many trading systems and timing indicators yield recommendations to buy or sell at the market. In such cases, the order is exactly what the system requires; you use an at-the-market order, which, as noted earlier, has its positive and negative aspects.

Systems That Buy or Sell on Breakouts

These systems generate orders to buy on a stop or stop limit order above the market or sell on a stop or stop limit order below the market. Such systems are categorized as breakout systems, or volatility breakout systems. They define a given price area as being either resistance or support. If an SSF trades above the resistance point as determined by the system, then a long position is established in the expectation that if the market trades above the resistance point, it is likely to continue higher. Alternatively, the expectation is that if a market trades below its support point, it is likely to continue lower.

In order to be prepared for all eventualities, some of these systems enter buy stop orders above the market and sell stop orders below the market. In other words, they "bracket the market" with two orders. If you use this strategy, make certain that you cancel one side of the order as soon as the other side gets filled unless you plan to use the other order as your stop loss. For example, consider the chart in Figure 10.1.

At points A and B, the system has identified two breakout points, one on the upside and one on the downside. Therefore, an order that would be placed as a sell stop order at B would be filled on the short side, and then the order at A would either remain as a stop loss or be canceled. The same procedure would take place at points C and D. In this case, point C was penetrated and the buy stop placed at C would have been filled on the opening of 29 July. The order at D would either remain as an open order sell stop to limit a loss, or it would be canceled.

▌ FIGURE 10.1 Breakout Points on Daily Chart

In this example, the orders used are buy stop, buy stop limit, buy stop with a limit, sell stop, sell stop limit, or sell stop with a limit (assuming that the given exchange accepts these orders). As you can readily see, it was the system or trading method that dictated the type of order to be used.

In the foregoing example, the system used was a volatility breakout system that traded consistently with the given market no matter which way it broke out. A similar approach could be used with a simple trend line breakout system as discussed in Chapter 7. See the illustration in Figure 10.2.

In this case (Figure 10.2), a penetration of the resistance trend line would have triggered a buy stop or a buy stop limit just above the trend line. A price fill would have taken place as the market penetrated the resistance line and would likely have been filled at point A or a little lower.

■ FIGURE 10.2 Buy Stop Executed in Trend Line Breakout Signal

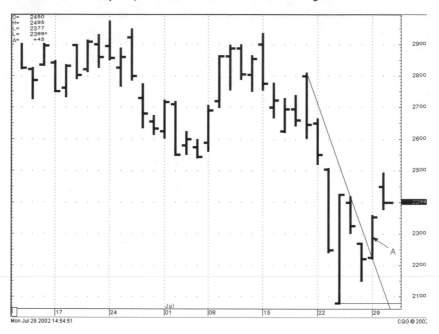

In Figure 10.3, a sell stop was executed at point A followed by a buy stop at point B. In each case the order used was a stop limit or a stop with a limit.

Support and Resistance Methods

Many technical traders use support and resistance methods as their approach to trading. Such methods first define a trend as either up, down, or sideways and then indicate buying at support in an up-trending market or selling at resistance in a downtrending market. In such cases, the method used dictates the type of order to be used. As an example, consider Figure 10.4, which illustrates an uptrend-ing market with support at the lower moving average line A and ini-tial support at the upper moving average line B. The object is to buy if and when prices decline to either or both of these levels and to take profits using another exit method. As you can see, by placing

FIGURE 10.3 Sell Stops Executed in Trend Line Breakout Signal

orders at the moving average values, long positions would have been established at points 1 through 5, which are declines to lower support. As noted, limit orders to buy would be used in this case.

There are many other systems for trading stocks, futures, and SSFs, but the general categories just described suffice for order placement in most cases.

▌ Placing a Hedge Order

As you know, one of the major uses of the SSF market is for placing a hedge. You will recall that when you place a hedge trade, you are trading against a position you already have. As an example, consider the following situation.

You are long 500 shares of IBM and want to protect your position by selling five contracts (500 shares) of IBM futures. Although you

■ FIGURE 10.4 Buying an SSF as Prices Decline to Support Using the 10 High/8 Low Moving Average Channel

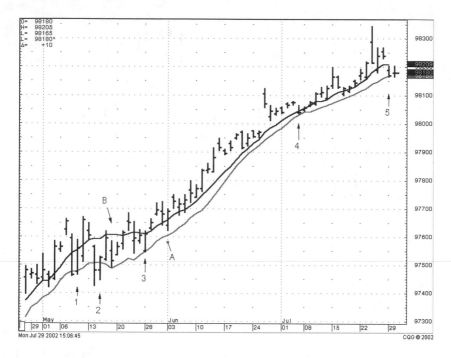

are indeed looking for the protection you want, you feel that the price of IBM has not yet reached its peak. For various reasons, you don't want to sell the stock when and if it hits a given price; instead, you want to sell an SSF contract and keep the stock. If the stock's price declines, you'll lose money on the stock but will make it back on the short SSF position. On the other hand, if IBM rises, then the SSF contract will lose money. This type of hedge is essentially similar to what farmers do when they hedge their crop or livestock production in the commodity markets. In this case, you would place a limit order above the market to sell short IBM futures. As soon as your price is touched, your order becomes a market order, you'll be short, and your two positions will be in balance. You make money on one, and you lose money on the other or vice versa. At some point in the future, you'll have the luxury of taking one or both sides of the hedge, and hopefully to your advantage on both sides.

▉ Summary

Other factors are to be considered in placing orders, some of which have been mentioned previously:

- Use market orders carefully.
- Avoid market orders in thinly traded markets.
- Remember to cancel orders when needed.
- Know which orders are accepted by the exchange.
- Have a backup system in the event that your electronic order-entry method fails.
- Evaluate bids and offers and use limit orders for position trading.
- Use market orders for day trading unless your system or method dictates otherwise.
- Monitor SSFs for trading volume in order to evaluate the potential use of market orders.
- Check with your broker or brokerage house if you are unclear about which orders you can or cannot use.
- When placing spread orders, be especially careful to enter the correct buy or sell order on the SSFs you want to trade as a spread.

CHAPTER ELEVEN

Advanced Technical Methods for SSFs

Although many trading systems and methods can be used for trading in SSFs, some clearly work better than others. This chapter provides an overview of indicators and methods that I have found particularly useful in the futures markets. In reviewing these indicators, you should bear in mind that systems and methods used for trading stocks are not necessarily effective or applicable to futures given the more volatile nature of the futures market, which, as you know, is a function of its lower margin.

■ The Gap Trade

The opening gap trade is a short-term trade that can be used effectively by day traders. The logic and rules of its application are not only simple but logical and sensible as well. The efficacy of the gap trade is based on trader psychology. The tendency of a stock or SSF contract to open below the previous day's session low or above the previous day's session high is a function of news that, in turn, prompts traders and investors to sell or buy aggressively. Hence, bearish news can cause an SSF market to open below the previous day's session low, whereas bullish news can cause an SSF market to open above the previous day's session high. Of course, the tendency of an SSF to act this way is a function of the behavior of the underlying stock.

As examples of gap higher and gap lower openings, examine Figures 11.1 and 11.2.

■ The Gap Trade Concept

Now that you can spot gap trades, this is the concept: When a market opens gap up (G+), there is a tendency for the price to retrace following the emotional buying that promoted the gap higher opening. If the price of the stock or SSF then falls below the high of the previous day, there is a tendency for the rest of the day to be lower and for the SSF to close lower than its open as well as lower than the high of the previous day, as illustrated in Figures 11.3 and 11.4.

At point 1 in Figure 11.3, NEM opened above the high of the previous day (point 2). It later dropped below point 2, giving a gap sell indication and close at point 3, lower than the price at which it triggered a sell pattern. At point A, prices opened above the previous daily high, B. Prices then declined to close at point C for a profitable day trade. At point D, prices opened above point E. When prices dropped below E, a short position would be entered and closed out at the end of the day, in this case, profitably.

Figure 11.4 shows the gap sell signal in NVDA. Note the gap higher open at A and penetration below the high of the day (A) and then the close well below the high of the day (A) at point B.

When a market opens gap down (G−), there is a tendency for the price to retrace following the emotional selling that promoted the gap lower opening. If the price of the stock or SSF contract then rallies above the low of the previous day, there is a tendency for the rest of the day to be higher and for the SSF contract to close higher than it opened as well as higher than the low of the previous day, as illustrated in Figures 11.5 and 11.6.

■ **FIGURE** 11.1 Gap Lower Openings in IBM (note – signs)

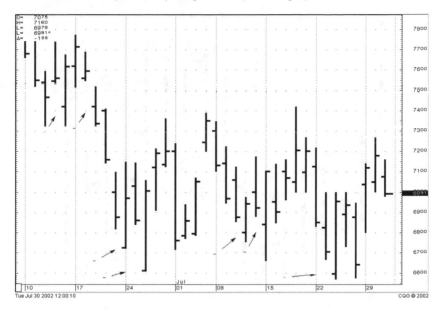

■ **FIGURE** 11.2 Gap Higher Openings in Kaufman and Broad (note + signs)

▌ FIGURE 11.3 The Gap Sell Trades in Newmont Mining (NEM)

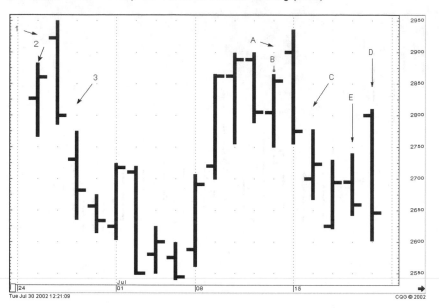

▌ FIGURE 11.4 Gap Sell Trade in NVDA

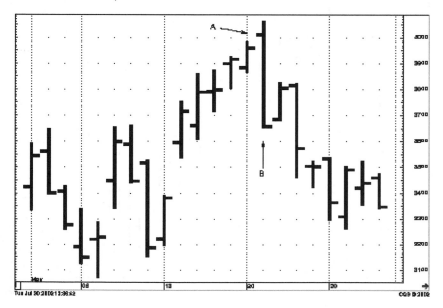

■ FIGURE 11.5 Gap Buy Signal in ADM. The lower open at A (i.e., below low B) resulted in a buy, which was closed out at C.

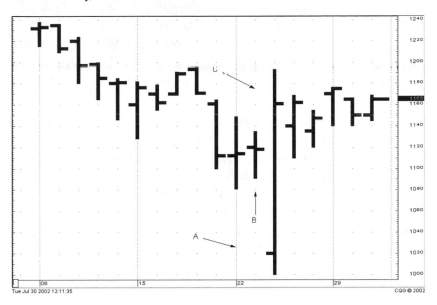

■ FIGURE 11.6 Gap Buy Signals on Days A and B

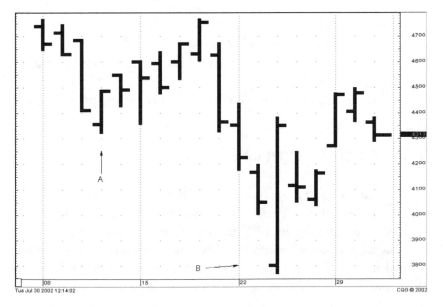

■ Trading Gaps

Although gaps don't occur often, they are very amenable to SSF trading. SSF gap trades are usually day trades, although you can hold until the next day. Take your time and study the gap trades. You may like what you see, particularly if you're a short-term trader. The rules for trading gaps in SSFs are simple. They are as follows:

- *If an SSF opens above the high of the previous day* by at least 5 percent of the previous daily trading range (i.e., high – low of day), then sell short on a penetration back below the high of the previous day.
- Use a risk management or dollar stop loss.
- Exit the trade at the end of the day.
- Use a trailing stop loss intraday if the position moves strongly in your favor.
- Consider trading multiple contracts and exiting on a scale up.

- *If an SSF contract opens on a gap below the low of the previous day* by 5 percent or more of the previous daily trading range, then sell short on a penetration back above the low of the previous day.
- Use a risk management or dollar stop loss.
- Exit the trade at the end of the day.
- Use a trailing stop loss intraday if the position moves strongly in your favor.
- Consider trading multiple contracts and exiting on a scale up.

■ Momentum Divergence

Momentum (also known as rate of change) is a powerful indicator, albeit one that has not been used very effectively by many traders. The difficulty in using the momentum indicator for timing SSF (as well as stock) trades is in its interpretation. This topic has been discussed extensively in my book *Momentum Stock Selection* (McGraw-Hill, 2000), in which I outline a number of steps for using momentum as a timing indicator in stocks. The use of momentum in SSFs is a natural extension of its use in stocks.

As noted by the heading of this section, momentum can be used to spot momentum divergence, which is simple to find but difficult for some traders to apply because they are not familiar with the correct timing application of momentum divergence. This section shows you how to use momentum divergence for timing SSF trades.

Definition

The momentum indicator compares the price of a given market today with the price X days ago. If the price today is higher than the price X days ago, then momentum is positive, or bullish. If the price of a market is lower than it was X days ago, then momentum is bearish. All you need to do to calculate momentum is subtract the closing price of a market today from the closing price X days ago if the price today was lower than the price X days ago. As an example, if the price today is 10 and the price X days ago was 20, then momentum for today is −10 (minus 10). If the price X days ago was 10 and the price today is 20, then momentum is +10 (plus 10). The X in this case is 28 periods. For a daily SSF price chart, the momentum would be determined using 28 days. For an hourly SSF chart, momentum would be determined using 28 periods of 60 minutes each.

Divergence

Divergence occurs when price and momentum are moving in opposite directions. In particular, when price is making a new low for a given period while momentum is moving higher, bullish divergence is occurring. When price is making a new high while momentum is moving lower, bearish divergence is said to be in process. Note that bullish and bearish divergence in and of themselves do not indicate that one should buy or sell. The divergence pattern must develop into a sell signal or a buy signal. Please refer to Figures 11.7 through 11.10 for examples of bullish and bearish divergence.

■ FIGURE 11.7 Bullish Divergence. Price low B was lower than price low A, while momentum C was higher than momentum D, thereby creating bullish divergence.

■ FIGURE 11.8 Bullish Divergence. Price low A was lower than price low C, while momentum low B was higher than momentum low D, thereby setting up bullish divergence.

▮ FIGURE 11.9 Bearish Divergence. Price high A was higher than price high C, while momentum at B was lower than momentum D, setting up bearish divergence.

▮ FIGURE 11.10 Bearish Divergence

The Key to Momentum Divergence

The key to using momentum divergence effectively in trading is timing. See Figures 11.11 through 11.14 for specific examples of buy and sell signals generated after momentum divergence patterns have developed.

Finding the Signals

Figures 11.11 through 11.14 illustrate buy and sell signals. As you can see, in the case of bullish divergence the momentum high (point E on Figures 11.13 and 11.14) is the buy points that, once penetrated, yield a buy signal. Figures 11.11 and 11.12 show bearish momentum divergence. Point E in this case is the sell point; once it has been penetrated, a sell signal develops. Remember that the momentum is what triggers a buy or a sell signal, not the price behavior of the SSF contract.

■ Momentum/Moving Average (MOM/MA)

Still another method of timing SSF trades is by using the momentum indicator (MOM) previously discussed with its moving average. The simple rules for this combination indicator are as follows:

- Calculate a 28-day momentum indicator.
- Calculate a 28-day moving average of the momentum indicator.
- When the 28-day momentum indicator rises above the 28-day moving average of the momentum indicator, a change in trend to the upside has likely started.
- When the 28-day momentum indicator falls below the 28-day moving average of the momentum indicator, a change in trend to the downside has likely started.
- Buy and sell signals are generated accordingly.

■ **FIGURE 11.11** Momentum Divergence Sell Signal. After setting up bearish divergence pattern A>C with B<D, a sell signal was triggered upon penetration of E.

■ **FIGURE 11.12** Momentum Divergence Sell Signal. After setting up bearish divergence at A>B and C<D, a sell signal was generated at penetration of E.

FIGURE 11.13 A momentum divergence buy signal will occur if point E is penetrated.

FIGURE 11.14 A momentum divergence buy signal occurs at penetration of point E.

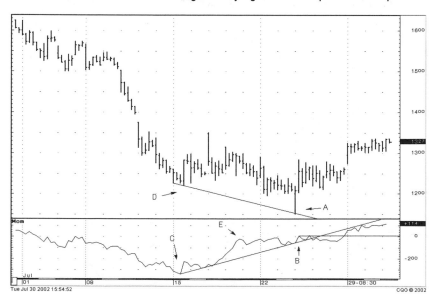

Figures 11.15 and 11.16 illustrate buy and sell signals, respectively, in a futures contract. Remember that this approach is not a trading system but rather a timing method. In order to function as a complete trading system, the method needs additional features, such as a risk management stop loss, added to it.

▌ FIGURE 11.15 Momentum/Moving Average (MOM/MA) Signals. This chart shows a buy signal at A and a sell signal at B.

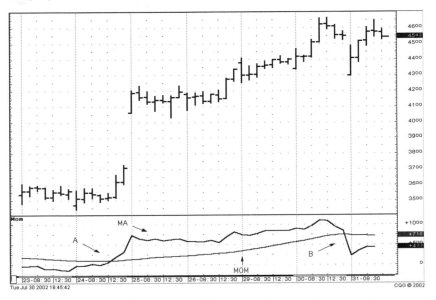

You can use this approach in trading SSF spreads as well as flat positions. This approach is also discussed in my book *Momentum Stock Selection* (McGraw-Hill, 2000).

■ **FIGURE 11.16** Momentum/Moving Average (MOM/MA) Signals. Note that two consecutive closes by the momentum above its MA signals a buy, whereas two consecutive closes below its MA signals a sell.

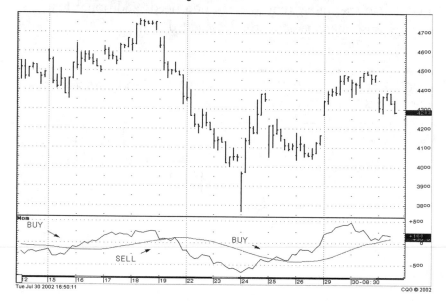

CHAPTER TWELVE

A Seasonal Strategy for SSFs

Seasonality is one of the most important underlying forces in the stock and futures markets. Although many traders, market analysts, and economists dispute the value—and even the existence—of seasonal forces in the markets, seasonal forces, or seasonals, do exist and do indeed account for certain trends within the course of the calendar year.

Art Merrill, for example, in his classic book *The Behavior of Prices on Wall Street* (Analysis Press, 1980) demonstrated the existence of preholiday behavior in the Dow Jones Industrial Average, concluding there was a high probability of higher closing prices in the Dow on the day before major U.S. holidays. His study demonstrated statistically that the odds of a chance occurrence in his findings were about 1 in 10,000!

My work in the futures markets also verifies the existence of seasonal patterns, which are often reflected in individual stocks as well as in the major stock indices.

As an example of such seasonal patterns, consider the tendency of the S&P 500 average to move higher from approximately January 12 through 18, a pattern that has been in existence for many years.

In fact, close examination of S&P futures from 1982 through 2001 (and well before 1982 in the cash S&P index) indicates a high probability of upward movement during this time frame.

Figure 12.1 shows a historical summary that illustrates my point about seasonality in the S&P 500 index. This summary shows hypothetical trading in S&P futures—buying on the close of trading January 12 every year from 1983 through 2001 and exiting the po-

---

▌ FIGURE 12.1 Key Date Seasonal Trade in S&P 500 Futures

MAR S&P 500 LONG Enter: 1/12 Exit: 1/18 Stop: 3 P/L Ratio: 1761.50 Trade #: 2197

ContractYr	Date In	Price In	Date Out	Price Out	Prof/Loss	Total
1983	1/12/83	147.950	1/18/83	148.350	0.400	0.400
1984	1/12/84	169.600	1/18/84	169.900	0.300	0.700
1985	1/14/85	173.350	1/18/85	173.400	0.050	0.750
1986	1/13/86	207.400	1/20/86	208.350	0.950	1.700
1987	1/12/87	260.750	1/19/87	271.400	10.650	12.350
1988	1/12/88	246.350	1/18/88	252.400	6.050	18.400
1989	1/12/89	285.250	1/18/89	288.700	3.450	21.850
1990	1/12/90	340.950	1/18/90	340.850	-0.100	21.750
1991	1/14/91	314.350	1/18/91	333.900	19.550	41.300
1992	1/13/92	415.800	1/20/92	417.400	1.600	42.900
1993	1/12/93	431.450	1/18/93	437.300	5.850	48.750
1994	1/12/94	474.200	1/18/94	474.400	0.200	48.950
1995	1/12/95	464.250	1/18/95	471.150	6.900	55.850
1996	1/12/96	604.950	1/18/96	610.500	5.550	61.400
1997	1/13/97	764.300	1/20/97	780.150	15.850	77.250
1998	1/12/98	945.500	1/20/98	985.200	39.700	116.950
1999	1/12/99	1251.100	1/19/99	1257.000	5.900	122.850
2000	1/12/00	1442.000	1/18/00	1469.500	27.500	150.350
2001	1/12/01	1330.300	1/18/01	1356.000	25.700	176.050

Trades: 19   Winners: 18   Losers: 1   %Winners: 94.73   Daily PF: 1.63

Avg Prof: 9.78   Avg Loss: -0.10   %Avg Prof: 1.64   %Avg Loss: -0.02

Copyright ©2002 MBH Commodity Advisors, Inc. 847-446-0800 1-800-678-5253

trade-futures.com

sition on the close of trading January 18 every year. For cases in which the market was closed on the ideal entry date, the trade would be executed on the close of business the next day; the trade carries a 3 percent closing basis stop loss.

As you can see, this pattern was correct well over 90 percent of the time during period shown. Naturally, a good statistician would argue that there were not enough trades in the sample to constitute a valid test of the pattern. If you look back prior to 1982, when S&P futures began trading, you'll find a similar pattern in the cash S&P 500, albeit with a lower but still significant percentage accuracy to the listing here shows. Seasonals are not perfect and some do indeed deteriorate over time, but in the main they are reliable and valid methods for trading.

Although literally hundreds of seasonal patterns exist in the major stock indices—some short-term, some longer-term—these patterns can be used successfully by traders who are aware of them and who, moreover, have the discipline to use them consistently.

As a further example, consider the seasonal patterns in the crude oil market shown in Figure 12.2.

It shows the seasonal pattern in fuel oil dating back to the 1930s. The line plot shows a strong tendency for prices to rise from August until late in the year. The up arrows show a high probability of an upward move for the month. The down arrows show a high probability of a downward move for the month. The bottom row shows the percentage of times the monthly average prices for the given month have been higher or lower for the period studied.

Based on the chart in Figure 12.2, you would expect to find a similar pattern in crude oil futures and, most likely, in petroleum stocks as well. Figure 12.3 shows the same pattern on a weekly basis in November crude oil futures. You can see the tendency for higher prices from late February through late August.

Based on the patterns illustrated in these studies, the odds are that a similar pattern would be found in petroleum company shares. Figure 12.4 shows the monthly prices of a major petroleum stock reflecting this seasonal pattern. Using this approach, trades could be made in SSFs or NBIs.

▌ FIGURE 12.2 Seasonal Tendency in Cash Fuel Oil, 1938–1997

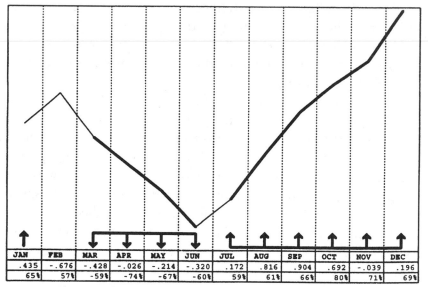

MONTHLY SEASONAL CASH ARRAY ANALYSIS: FUELOIL   YEARS: 1938 – 1997

	JAN	FEB	MAR	APR	MAY	JUN	JUL	AUG	SEP	OCT	NOV	DEC
JAN	57%	-52%	-57%	-55%	-55%	-57%	-54%	50%	54%	56%	57%	
FEB		-59%	-70%	-75%	-72%	-74%	-67%	-61%	-56%	-56%	-54%	
MAR			-74%	-71%	-68%	-68%	-64%	-59%	50%	55%	53%	
APR				-67%	-67%	-64%	-58%	-52%	52%	56%	59%	
MAY					-60%	-53%	52%	55%	62%	64%	70%	
JUN						59%	59%	64%	72%	73%	78%	
JUL							61%	64%	74%	81%	73%	
AUG								66%	78%	79%	75%	
SEP									80%	76%	73%	
OCT										71%	71%	
NOV											69%	

MONTHLY SEASONAL CASH TENDENCY: FUELOIL   YEARS: 1938 – 1997

IDEAL SEASONAL HIGH MONTH : DEC   HIGH % SEASONAL UP   MONTHS : JAN JUL AUG SEP OCT
IDEAL SEASONAL LOW MONTH : JUN   HIGH % SEASONAL DOWN MONTHS : MAR APR MAY JUN

JAN	FEB	MAR	APR	MAY	JUN	JUL	AUG	SEP	OCT	NOV	DEC
.435	-.676	-.428	-.026	-.214	-.320	.172	.816	.904	.692	-.039	.196
65%	57%	-59%	-74%	-67%	-60%	59%	61%	66%	80%	71%	69%

▌ Other Timing Systems and Methods

The availability of low-cost computers, historical data, and advanced analytical programs allows contemporary traders to develop, test, and refine a literally unlimited number of trading systems or

■ FIGURE 12.3 Seasonal Tendency in November Crude Oil Futures

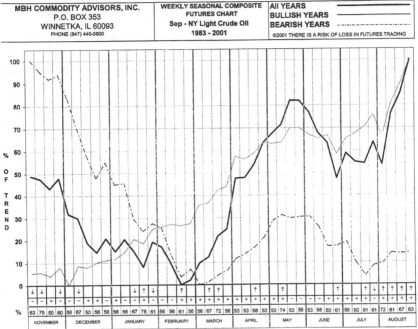

MBH COMMODITY ADVISORS, INC. P.O. BOX 353 WINNETKA, IL 60093 PHONE (847) 446-0800	WEEKLY SEASONAL COMPOSITE FUTURES CHART Sep - NY Light Crude Oil 1983 - 2001	All YEARS ———————— BULLISH YEARS ———————— BEARISH YEARS ------------ ©2001 THERE IS A RISK OF LOSS IN FUTURES TRADING

methods. Yet in spite of these advances, most traders still lose. Even though the SSF market offers many new opportunities to traders and investors, far too many adventurers in this market will lose money. Three essential reasons account for this sad state of affairs:

1. Most traders fail to adequately pretest trading systems and timing indicators before using them.
2. Most traders overoptimize trading systems, thus creating systems that perform exceptionally well in pretesting but, because of their curve-fitted nature, fail to perform profitably in real-time applications. Curve fitting is the process of adjusting a trading system to perform well on historical data. Curve-fitted systems tend to fail in the future.
3. Most traders lack the self-discipline and winning psychology to consistently apply their methods to the markets.

■ **FIGURE 12.4** Seasonal Price Pattern in a Petroleum Stock. Arrows up show seasonal rallies in this petroleum stock. The arrow down shows a contraseasonal decline.

To avoid becoming a statistic in the SSF market, I recommend the following general rules for trading systems and timing methods. Please take them seriously. I have learned them through lengthy and often painful experiences:

- Your trading system or timing method must be one with which you are comfortable, so you'll apply it consistently without second-guessing.
- Your trading system or method should ideally be based on a concept or concepts that have some degree of validity.
- Your trading system or method must represent the worst-case scenarios in pretesting as opposed to best-case results. I say this because the reality of the marketplace is that the worst case develops more often than the best case. Showing worst-case

results historically will temper your optimism, melding firmly with realistic expectations as opposed to dreams of perfection.

- Make certain that the timing method or system you use provides clear-cut rules of application that, by their nature, eliminate the need for interpretation and/or guessing.
- Consider using a different method for exiting trades than the one that was used for entering trades.
- Consider different indicators for long and short positions.
- If your trading decisions are currently based on fundamentals alone, then consider adding timing to the mix to improve the results.
- If your trading decisions are currently based exclusively on timing and technical factors, you may want to add some general fundamentals into the plan to improve the longer-term perspective.
- Consider adding contrary opinion indicators into your trading plan, as futures tend to be more responsive to trader sentiment than are stocks. (See Chapter 13.)
- Remember that systems that were effective for stocks may not necessarily be effective in the SSF markets and vice versa.
- Develop a system or method for trading SSF spreads. This area could offer some of the largest rewards with the lowest amount of risk.
- Study timing oscillators, such as moving average convergence/divergence (MACD) for short-term swing trading.
- Investigate more complex methodologies, such as combinations of SSF futures and stock options.

CHAPTER THIRTEEN

The Psychology of Single Stock Futures

The adjustment that may be required in moving from trading stocks exclusively to also trading SSFs, as well as the move from trading futures exclusively to also trading SSFs, could very well require a considerable adjustment in perspective, perception, and psychology. The psychological makeup of most traders is often tenuous even in the traditional markets. Adding SSFs into the trading plan may not only require a new view of the markets but could also significantly increase traders' stress levels. Why? Many traders are concerned about "missing out on the trading action," fearing they'll be left behind. They fear losing their advantage to other traders by not having sufficient knowledge or experience. And all of these fears could easily affect trader psychology that, as previously stated, is often already fragile.

I could tell you many things about different trading systems and methods that can be used in SSF trading, along with the lessons I've learned through long and hard experience, but none of them would be more meaningful than the lessons I've learned about *discipline, organization,* and *psychology.* The suggestions and directions I am able to give you about these three important areas for realizing success in futures trading are the most important information I can provide. In fact, this could be the most important chapter in the entire book.

I maintain that the single most important variable for success in futures trading is not the trading system you are using. Furthermore, the speed of your computer, the inside information you have, the amount of trading capital you use, or the broker with whom you are trading are not significant if your psychology is faulty. What eventually separates winners from losers—commercial, speculative, short-term, long-term, or otherwise—is *discipline* in its many aspects and at its many levels.

■ The Persistence of Old Issues

To most traders, discipline is just another effete topic that is all too often overlooked or rejected as a result of its familiarity. Yet in no way does this minimize its importance. Although we have all heard the words and the warnings; although we may have studied the rules and the teachings; although we may believe that there is value in following the rules of self-discipline, we still tend to make mistakes in applying these rules. My observations and experiences in the futures markets and with futures traders lead me to the solid conclusion that the lessons have not been learned by far too many traders. I hope the information and advice in this chapter will assist you.

■ Can Trading Discipline Be Learned?

The word *discipline* signifies something traders know they have to develop, and they often, although incorrectly, believe they have no problems with discipline. In their heart of hearts, however, most traders know they are severely lacking in discipline and that they will probably never have it. And this is a sad situation indeed, because I believe that discipline can be learned. However, it takes effort, practice, and persistence.

Although some traders believe that discipline is virtually impossible to teach or to learn, they are incorrect. Because the topic of discipline is complex, elusive, evasive, and often camouflaged, it is difficult to learn and, moreover, to internalize. Nonetheless, it is the *sine qua non* of success in virtually every form of human effort, in every field of achievement, and in every generation. But to the best of my knowledge, there is no simple way to define discipline.

Adding to the problem is that many futures traders have virtually no objective trading system but, through the application and development of discipline, have achieved success. On the other hand, many futures traders use excellent trading systems but still lack the discipline to be successful. What frustrates them, adding to their woes, is that in spite of compelling statistical evidence supporting the validity of their systems, they still fail to generate profits in real time. Discipline can transform a marginally successful trading system into a highly profitable one. Lack of discipline, on the other hand, can degrade a potentially successful trading system into a losing proposition.

The purpose of this chapter is twofold: First, to emphasize the importance of discipline as a key element for success in any market; and, second, to suggest a number of ways in which discipline can be developed and improved. Let's first examine how discipline functions as well as its critical importance in the development and maintenance of a profitable trading methodology.

In the Eyes of Discipline: SSFs Not Unique

Although the SSF as a trading instrument is unique and unprecedented, another aspect of SSFs is not at all unique. SSFs are subject to the same limitations as are all forms of trading. By limitations I mean that trader error is more of a limiting factor than is a trading system or method. Even though SSF trading may offer new and exciting profit possibilities, this potential is limited by the weakest link in the chain, which is, and has always been, the trader.

■ How Discipline Impacts Profits

There are literally thousands of approaches to futures trading. Some are potentially more profitable than others; some are simple and easily applied, whereas others are complex; some are logical and some not so logical. Regardless of the trading approach one employs, all trading systems and methods have certain elements in common. Three of these are as follows:

1. Specific signals (rules) for determining entry and exit of long and short positions as well as stop losses and trailing stop losses (where used).
2. Specific parameters and methods of calculating timing signals that are consistent, operational, and capable of being replicated by other traders with access to the same information and methods.
3. Specific trading actions and procedures that must be implemented as a function of information generated by points 1 and 2.

When systems and methods are tested by computer to generate hypothetical or ideal results, they are often not validated in real time before being implemented. In such an artificial situation—one that assumes perfect compliance to the trading rules that have been programmed into the computer—the results will reflect perfection. What is tested historically by computer is completely consistent, because it is implemented by a computer that follows instructions without fail. The output of such a test consists of a listing of trades and hypothetical results based on the aforementioned perfect execution of the rules that were programmed into the computer. But the computer is not a human, subject to fear, greed, lack of funds, lack of belief, and other limiting factors.

The output of the system test yields a wealth of objective information, including such statistics as the percentage of profitable trades, the percentage of unprofitable trades, the percentage of trades that break even, the average winning trade in dollars, the average losing trade in dollars, the performance for given markets, and the average length of time per trade. All data derived from the computer test of a trading model are based on flawless follow-up, implementation, and execution of trading signals according to the parameters programmed into the computer.

Some systems are profitable 55 to 65 percent of the time, whereas others show much higher percentages of profitability. But statistics can be misleading: I have rarely seen systems that are profitable more than 80 percent of the time. As you can imagine, a trading system that is correct 90 percent of the time, making a $100 profit on the average each time and then losing $900 on the occasion that it is wrong, would certainly not be very profitable. Furthermore, the individual trading this system would lose on one large losing trade all the profits made on nine trades! One losing trade would bring the account back to even. Should there be another error because of a lack of discipline, the account would show a net loss.

Conversely, a trading system may show eight losers for every two winners. If, however, the average profitable trade is much larger than the average losing trade, even a system having nine losers out of every ten trades could be profitable if the bottom line per trade were higher on the winning side. Nevertheless, such a system would be thrown astray if lack of discipline resulted in much larger losses than expected for the eight losing trades. If lack of discipline interfered significantly with the profits on the two profitable trades, then the net results might be much worse than anticipated.

A third scenario would be a marginal trading system. Assume a trading system is profitable about 65 percent of the time. In such cases, we can figure that approximately 65 out of every 100 trades are winners and 35 are losers. You can see that only 30 percent separates the winners from the losers. In other words, the trader must have sufficient discipline to keep the losses as small as possible and to maximize profits. This is where discipline enters into the formula for success.

Discipline is the machinery that can make or break any trading system. Some conditions do occur under which discipline will not be the important variable, although it *is* the significant variable in most cases. All the glowing statistics for your trading system will be totally useless if you're not capable of duplicating the exact statistics generated by the computer test of your trading system. In other words, you must stick as close to the averages as possible, or else one or two losses much larger than the average or one or two profits much smaller than the average will be sufficient to ruin your results.

Sometimes this can occur strictly as a function of market behavior (i.e., limit moves against you). However, more often than not, as I have stated before, it is the trader who is responsible for maintaining the discipline of a system.

■ Staying Up-to-Date—Another Form of Discipline

It is uncanny how many times markets will begin major moves in line with the expectations of many advisors, analysts, and speculators, who fail to be aboard for the big move. Why does this happen? How often has this happened to you? I know from personal experience that many individuals have good records at predicting where prices will go. I also know they have especially poor records when it comes to doing their homework, as explained in the following section.

Defining "Homework"

What do I mean by doing your "homework"? I simply mean keeping up to date on the signals generated by the system or systems you are following. To keep in touch with the markets according to your system, you need a regular schedule for doing the technical or fundamental work your system requires. Whether this work consists of simple charting that may take only five minutes a day or complex mathematical calculations that may take considerably longer, the discipline of doing your homework is one of the prerequisites for successful trading.

If you have a system but don't follow it, you are guilty of poor discipline. If you have a system but fail to do the work necessary to generate your trading signals, then you are just as guilty of lacking discipline. As you can see, and as you can well appreciate, most traders don't even get beyond the first step.

Can you identify strongly, or even partially, with some of the things I'm saying? How often have you missed a move because your charts or systems were not up to date? How many times has this frus-

trated you into making an unwarranted decision in an effort to compensate for your first error? The truth is that many of us are guilty of
these lapses in judgment. Sadly, rectifying these lapses is a very simple matter. In fact, the steps you must take to rectify virtually any
problem resulting from lack of trading discipline are very specific,
easily understood, and exceptionally elementary to implement.

The discipline required to trade consistently and successfully is
the same type of discipline required in virtually every aspect of
human life. Whether it is the discipline required to lose weight,
stop smoking, or develop a successful business, the basics of all discipline are the same.

If you develop discipline in your trading, I'm certain it will spread
to other areas of your life, including your personal affairs.
Unfortunately, however, discipline in other aspects of your life may
not necessarily spread very quickly to your trading. The nature of
futures trading provides serious challenges to discipline developed
in other areas of life. Suggestions for improving discipline are provided later in this chapter.

The Chronic Lack of Discipline

Lack of discipline is not confined to any one situation, any one
trade, or any one trader; it is a way of life, albeit a nonproductive one.
Individuals who achieve success without adhering to certain disciplined practices do so as a stroke of good fortune and chance forfeit-
ing their wealth through a lack of disciplined action. Unfortunately,
the lack of discipline is not a simple matter but instead spreads like a
cancerous growth throughout a trader's behavior. In an interpersonal
relationship, lack of discipline and specificity can cause negative interaction, which in turn results in further tests of discipline and self-
control. And these tests, in turn, result in other problems—failures
and negative experiences—until the entire relationship is threatened. The same holds true for trading.

Lack of discipline in instituting a trade may frustrate a trader into
a further display of poor discipline. After several such incidents, the
trader will become frustrated, leading to the likelihood of further

errors. The net result is usually a succession of errors, each compounding the next one and thus likely to be far worse than the previous one. For this reason, a trader must take great care to avoid making the first mistake stemming from a lack of discipline. The first mistake leads to the second; the second may lead to 4 others; and 4 others may lead to 16 others. This is the manner in which a lack of discipline tends to spread or become chronic.

■ How to Improve Your Discipline

I don't have all the answers to how you can improve your discipline, but I do have a number of cogent, time-tested techniques that may help. All of my suggestions require action and thorough implementation if they are to have a beneficial effect on your results.

1. Make a schedule and follow it. To help you keep your trading signals and systems current, set aside a given time of the day or week during which you will do the necessary calculations, charts, or other market work. Doing the same work every day of the week helps you get into a specific routine, which in turn eliminates the possibility (or greatly reduces it) of not being prepared when a major move develops.

2. Don't try to trade too many SSFs. Attempt to specialize in one particular trading approach. If you try to trade in too many SSFs or with too many systems at one time, your work will become a burden, you won't look forward to it, and you'll be more prone to let your studies fall behind. The ideal is to seek to work in no more than three to five markets at any given time and attempt to specialize in only one system.

3. Use a checklist. One of my favorite analogies is that between the trader and the airplane pilot. Before takeoff a good airplane pilot goes through his preflight checklist. I certainly wouldn't want to fly in a plane with a pilot who was sloppy in this procedure—would you?

The trader who wishes to eliminate trading errors should also maintain a checklist, consulting it regularly, preferably before each trade is made. Of all of my suggestions, the checklist is probably the best one for all traders. I would suggest that even after your checklist has become automatic, you still maintain it, because lack of discipline is likely to attack you at almost any time. Not only can it strike without notice but it often does.

4. Don't accept third-party input once your decision has been made. I have come to respect the fact that good traders are usually loners. They must do their work in isolation, and they must implement their decisions in isolation. A pushy or talkative broker, a well-intentioned friend, or a very persuasive newsletter writer can often sway you from a decision that only you should make. There are times when your decision will be wrong, but these are part of the learning experience, and you alone must make your decisions based on the facts as you see them.

If you have decided to follow your own trading system, then by all means follow it and forget about other input. If, however, your system is based on input from other sources, then try to implement your decisions without being swayed from them once your mind has been made up. The benefits of deciding on your own far outweigh the potential benefits of having too much input.

5. Evaluate your progress. Feedback is a crucial part of the learning process. Keep track of how you are doing with your trading, not only in terms of dollars and cents, but also in terms of specific signals, behavior, and techniques. This gives you an idea of how closely you are staying with the rules, which rules you are breaking, and how often you may be breaking them.

It is important to know when you make mistakes, but it is more important to know what kinds of mistakes you make and how often you make them. This will help you overcome the lack of discipline that causes trading errors to occur.

6. Learn from every loss. Losses are tuition—expensive and good for something. Learn from each loss and do your very best to avoid taking the same loss twice or more for the same reason. Do not repeat the same errors. To do so indicates that your discipline is not improving.

7. Understand yourself. This is certainly a big job and not one easily accomplished. It is extremely important that you understand your motivation and your true reasons for trading the markets. Frequently, individuals do poorly in the markets because their objectives and goals are not well established initially. Self-understanding helps clarify your personal goals and thereby makes the process of attaining your goals more specific.

8. Improve your trading system and remain dedicated to it. If you are like most traders, you will have done considerable research on a trading method or system. Some traders, however, become quickly disenchanted with their system and hop from one technique to another. This is one of the worst forms of poor discipline because it doesn't allow a system sufficient time to perform. By hopping from one system to another, the speculator takes considerably more overall risk than she should.

9. Clarify and frequently restate your objectives. At times, poor training discipline can be a function of unclear objectives. If you have decided that you want to trade for the short term only, then you have a very clear objective. However, if you aren't certain about the time frame of your trading, about the trading system you plan to use as your vehicle, about the relationship you wish to have with your broker, about the quotation equipment you plan to use (if any), then you are prone to mistakes and poor discipline.

My suggestion is to make all major trading decisions before you even get started with your trading. Some corrections can be made along the way, but a majority of decisions must be made prior to any serious trading.

10. Know when you are wrong. In order to improve your trading discipline, it is important to have an objective measure of when you will terminate a given trade, profitably or unprofitably. Whether this is done at a particular price or at a particular dollar amount is of no consequence, but you must know when you have had enough.

11. Make commitments and keep them. It is important in trading to make and keep commitments in the markets just as it is in every phase of human endeavor and interaction. If, however, you do not make a commitment or if the commitment you make is not clear, then you stand the chance of not following through on an important phase of your trading. For this reason, I encourage all traders to make specific commitments, not only in terms of such things as trading systems, trading approach, available capital, or maximum risk, but also in terms of each and every trade they make.

Don't make the trade unless you are fully committed to it. What does this mean? It means that many individuals are prone to establish a position in the market based on what "looks like" a good signal or when it "looks like the market wants to turn higher." In other words, halfhearted and partial commitments are made on the basis of vague indications.

To make a commitment that will serve you well, don't make one based on sketchy information. The uneasy feeling you get when you make such a decision will be enough to let you know that you are not making a commitment based on correct procedures.

Many more ways to improve your discipline could be listed, but quite a few of these are probably specific to your individual situation. One good way in which to determine how, where, when, and what type of commitment you wish to make is to examine yourself, using a checklist or questionnaire designed to ascertain the precise nature of your situation. Ordinarily, this can be done with only a brief amount of thought and analysis.

■ Summary

Success in the SSF markets will not come easily no matter how good your system or trading method may be. There will be successes and there will be failures. Failures will often cost you more total money than you'll gain in total profits if you lack the discipline to follow a systematic trading approach. With the possible exception of persistence, discipline is the single most important quality a trader can possess. Though discipline cannot be taught or learned in a classroom, traders can do many things to facilitate the learning process. This chapter discussed the relevant aspects of discipline and suggested how your discipline might be improved. Follow these suggestions and you will succeed in the SSF market as well as in other forms of trading and investing.

CHAPTER FOURTEEN

Day Trading Single Stock Futures

Since the mid to late 1980s, several diverse but related factors have combined to create a market environment that has been highly conducive for day trading. These factors are:

- The low (and declining) cost of powerful computer systems required to test and maintain technical trading systems and on-line order entry software
- Affordable trading software
- Affordable real-time price quotations (i.e., live tick-by-tick data)
- The availability of Level II quotations
- The relatively low cost of trading commissions
- The ability to enter and execute orders electronically for prompt execution

Combined with increased trading volume and the globalization of markets, opportunities for the day trader abound. Yet, day trading has not been the golden opportunity that so many traders and brokerage firms had expected or predicted. The sad but true fact is that bull markets tend to be favored by most investors, due not only to the fact that selling short is often more risky than buying but also to the fact that there are limitations on how short sales are executed (i.e., an uptick is required in a stock before a short sale can be filled). Since the bull market top of 2000, day traders have been in especially dire straits given their typically bullish orientation. Many day traders who made large profits in the seemingly endless bull market of the mid to late 1990s have given back their profits (and more) in the bear market of the early 2000s.

Despite advances in technology, despite low commissions, despite the speed of electronic order entry, and despite the low cost of computers, day traders have suffered in the bear market due, in part, to their frequently bullish bias but also to the typical problems of self-discipline that afflict so many traders. Still, day trading holds a particular fascination for many investors. Based on my research in the stock and futures markets, I conclude that day trading is not only a viable undertaking but also a desirable one for individuals who have not developed either the patience or the investing strategies to hold stocks for the long term. Before you reject the possibility of day trading in the SSF market, consider the potential benefits of being a day trader as outlined in Figure 14.1.

■ Other Aspects of Day Trading

Yes, there are also negatives to day trading. The most significant of these is the tendency of undisciplined traders to turn a losing day trade into an "investment" by failing to exit the trade by the end of the day. This is, of course, a shortcoming of discipline rather than a shortcoming of day trading itself. As long as day traders follow a well-thought-out plan with discipline and effective risk management, the odds of success can be quite good, provided that the market environment is conducive to day trading. What I'm saying is simply that not all types of markets are day trading "friendly." Day traders who learned their craft in bull markets have been trained in a fashion that will not serve them well in bear markets—or, for that matter, in sideways ("choppy") markets.

■ **FIGURE 14.1** The Positive Aspects of Day Trading

- No need to be concerned about overnight news affecting your stock holdings.
- You know the "score" at the end of each day—win, lose, or break even.
- Your capital can "work" for you more efficiently if your trading is prof-itable.
- There are numerous, effective techniques that can be used for day trading. By being out at the end of each day, you will avoid riding losses.
- It is easier to be correct for a short-term move than for a long-term move.
- You can take advantage of ultra-short-term swings.
- You can trade more actively, thereby taking advantage of more op-portunities.

The SSF market is fertile ground for day traders inasmuch as the 20 percent margin provides excellent leverage. When compared to the approximate 1 percent margin in traditional futures, 20 percent may seem rather large; however, the benefit of larger margins is less volatility. While the 20 percent margin is considerably higher than the 1 percent in traditional futures, it still offers considerable lever-age for the day trader, while reducing the volatility and, therefore, also reducing the risk.

The purpose of this chapter is to familiarize you with several more day trading methods that have merit in the SSF market (see Chapter 11 for the "gap method" of day trading). I originally devel-oped these techniques for the traditional futures markets, but I be-lieve that they can be used in the SSF market as well, perhaps with even better results because of the higher margin requirement. I will discuss, in detail, three specific methods for day trading SSFs.

■ Surfing the Moving Average Channel

You should already be familiar with my use of the moving average channel (MAC) as discussed in Chapter 8. The method is a simple one. Most of the available trading software packages can display the MAC. Here is a review of how the MAC works for position trading:

- Use a 10-period simple moving average of the highs (MAH).
- Use an 8-period simple moving average of the lows (MAL).
- Two consecutive price bars entirely *above* the MAC constitutes a change in trend from down to up and a buy signal.
- Two consecutive price bars entirely *below* the MAC constitutes a change in trend from up to down and a sell signal.
- Use a dollar risk stop, a percentage of price entry stop, or reverse positions when the trend changes (as defined above).

Figure 14.2 illustrates this approach on a stock.

As you can see, there was a sell signal in mid-June, following which the market declined considerably. A low was made and a buy signal developed in mid-August. The trend thereafter continued higher as prices found support at the MAC.

■ FIGURE 14.2 The Moving Average Channel Illustrated

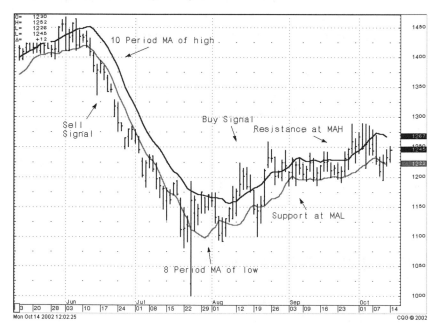

In this case, the chart shows daily price bars; however, the same rules can be applied to intraday price bars using the same rules as cited earlier. Figure 14.3 shows the same methodology applied to an intraday chart of EBAY.

At point A in Figure 14.3, a buy signal developed. A strong rally followed. The day trade would have been exited on the close at point B for a profit. As you can also see from this chart, prices continued to find support at the MAL after the original buy signal at point A.

▮ Channel Surfing

In addition to the above-mentioned trading method using the MAC, there is another approach that offers excellent potential to the SSF trader. This approach, affectionately termed "channel surfing," uses the same basic rules but with a significant variation on the theme. Here are the rules of application:

▮ FIGURE 14.3 10-Minute Chart of EBAY Showing MAC Signals

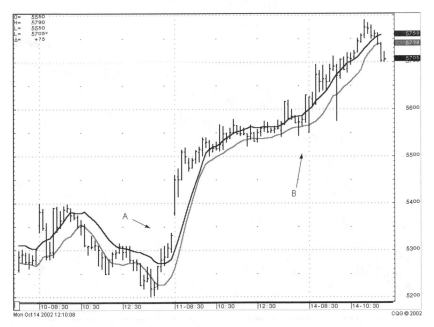

- Use a 10-period simple moving average of the highs (MAH).
- Use an 8-period simple moving average of the lows (MAL).
- Two consecutive price bars entirely *above* the MAC constitutes a change in trend from down to up and a buy signal.
- Two consecutive price bars entirely *below* the MAC constitutes a change in trend from up to down and a sell signal.
- In an uptrend (as defined above), you can *buy* when prices decline to the MAL and exit at the MAH for a short-term trade.
- In a downtrend (as defined above), you can *sell* short when prices rally to the MAH and exit at the MAL for a short-term trade.
- Use a dollar risk stop, a percentage of price entry stop, or reverse positions when the trend changes (as defined above).

Figure 14.4 illustrates the channel surfing approach described above.

As you can readily see from this chart, there were five long side entry points (i.e., buying at the MAL) and five exit points at the MAH. Of the five buy points, four were potentially profitable.

■ FIGURE 14.4 Channel Surfing in the Day Time Frame

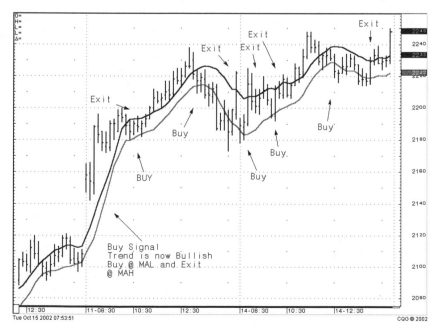

Furthermore, the original buy signal remained in effect for the entire two-day period, resulting in a much larger overall profit than the channel surfing day trades.

Comments about the Channel Surfing Method

As you can see from my several examples, using the MAC with the ten high and eight low parameters can yield profitable day trading results; however, in order to use this approach effectively and consistently, you will need to remember and implement the following salient aspects of this methodology:

- Select SSFs that are reasonably volatile. Because your profits with a channel surf trade are limited to the width of the MAC, you will need to trade SSFs that have reasonable trading ranges. If the MAC is narrow (i.e., the difference between the MAH and the MAL is small), then your profit potential will be limited. A wide channel is preferable.
- Use a risk management procedure to take you out of your trades when they have gone against you by more than a certain dollar amount or by more than a certain percentage move. The amount you select should be large enough to give the market room to move, but small enough to limit your losses to a reasonable amount. If your risk amount is too small, then you will be stopped out repeatedly and the method will not work for you. The correct stop loss or risk amount should be a function of the SSF, underlying market conditions, and the degree of risk you are willing to accept within the constraints of your account size.
- If you use the channel surfing method for day trading, then be sure to follow through by exiting your trades by the end of the day.
- Consider using multiple contracts, so that you can exit a portion of your position at the profit target (i.e., the MAH or the MAL), while maintaining the balance of your position for a larger move with a trailing stop loss.
- The channel surfing method *cannot* be used for intraday spread trading, because calculating the high and low of a

spread by using the intraday prices does not accurately reflect the actual trading price of a spread.

- You can channel surf in a different time frame. For day trading SSFs, I recommend no less than the 5-minute time frame; however, my preference is for 10-minute price bars in higher volatility SSFs and 30-minute price bars in less volatile SSFs and market conditions. The number of potential day trade opportunities is a function of the bar length you use. In other words, if you use 5-minute bars, you will have many more trades than if you use 10-minute or 30-minute bars.

- Remember that in day trading your expectation should be to capture small moves with high accuracy. In order to make the overall procedure profitable, you will need to trade larger positions (i.e., more contracts) than you would for position trades.

■ The 30-Minute Breakout

Another method for day trading SSFs is to use the 30-minute breakout method that I originally developed for trading the traditional futures markets. The approach is very simple. Here are the rules:

- Use 30-minute price bars.
- Buy on any 30-minute *close above* the high of the first 30-minute bar.
- Sell short on any 30-minute *close below* the low of the first 30-minute bar.
- Exit on opposite signal (i.e., if you go long first and then a short sell signal occurs, reverse your position and vice versa).
- If not stopped out, then exit on the close of the day.
- Use a trailing stop once your position is profitable.

As an example of this method, see Figure 14.5. It illustrates the above points in chart form.

As you can see, sell signals were triggered every day early in the trading session, with an exit at the end of each day. Note that I have

■ FIGURE 14.5 30-Minute Breakout Sell Signals

drawn a horizontal line using the high of the first 30-minute bar. When this line is penetrated on a 30-minute closing basis (i.e., at the end of the bar), a sell signal occurs.

Conversely, buy signals develop when the high of the first 30-minute bar is penetrated at the end of any subsequent 30-minute time frame. Buy signals are illustrated in Figure 14.6.

Here are a few considerations to take into account when using the 30-minute breakout in trading the SSF market:

- Trade active SSFs only, because low volume markets create more false signals.
- Trade SSFs that are more volatile (i.e., larger trading range), because the profit potential will be larger.
- As in the case of all day trades, be certain to close out your positions by the end of the day or they will not be day trades.
- You *cannot* use the 30-minute breakout method for day trading spreads.

▮ FIGURE 14.6 30-Minute Breakout Buy Signals

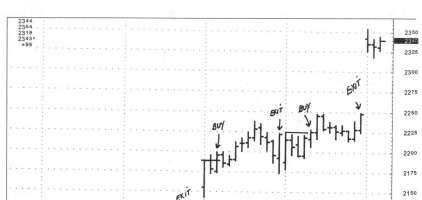

- Once you have a profit on your 30-minute breakout trade(s), use a trailing stop loss or a break-even stop loss to limit your risk.
- Consider trading several contracts, with a different exit strategy for each determined by market conditions.
- In the case of lower-priced SSFs, consider a larger position in order to compensate for the smaller size of the moves.
- In the event that your first signal of the day is incorrect, take the next trade in the opposite direction but limit yourself to two trades a day (i.e., first the buy and then the sell, or first the sell and then the buy) in order to avoid "whipsaws" that can occur on trendless days.
- Exit your trades by the end of the day using a market on close (MOC) order, if such an order is permitted.
- If you have a large profit toward the end of the day, consider exiting before the end of the day, particularly if the market begins to head in the opposite direction of your position.

References

Bernstein, Jacob. *The Investor's Quotient*. 2nd ed. Wiley, 1993.

———. *The Compleat Day Trader*. McGraw-Hill, 1995.

———. *Seasonality: Systems, Strategies and Signals*. Wiley, 1998.

———. *The Compleat Day Trader II*. McGraw-Hill, 1998.

———. *Momentum Stock Selection*. McGraw-Hill, 2000.

———. *The Compleat Guide to Day Trading Stocks*. McGraw-Hill, 2000.

———. *Strategies for the Electronic Futures Trader*. McGraw-Hill, 2000.

———. *Profit in the Futures Markets*. Bloomberg Press, 2002.

Edwards, Robert D., and John Magee. *Technical Analysis of Stock Trends*. 6th ed. NYIF, 1992.

Fink, Robert E., and Robert B. Feduniak. *Futures Trading: Concepts and Strategies*. NYIF, 1988.

Murphy, John J. *Technical Analysis of the Futures Markets*. NYIF, 1986.

Schwager, Jack D. *Schwager on Futures: Technical Analysis*. Wiley, 1996.

<www.onechicago.com>

<www.trade-futures.com>

Glossary

arbitrage (arbing, arbitraging) The simultaneous purchase of one market against the sale of another in order to profit from distortions and differences in normal and typical price relationships. Variations include simultaneous purchase and sale of different delivery months of the same market, of the same commodity and delivery month on two different exchanges, and the purchase of one market against the sale of another market. See also *spread*.

back month A calendar month that is active and more than 90 days away from the current trading month. This term is sometimes used to signify a month in which futures trading is taking place with a maturity other than the current trading month.

bar chart A graph of horizontal bars or vertical columns comparing characteristics of two or more items or showing differing proportions of those items. Bar charts are used in technical analysis to track price ranges and movements.

bear market A market that retreats 20 percent from its previous high.

bid/offer A bid is an offer to buy at a given price; an offer is an order to sell at a given price. Buyers bid for a given contract, and sellers offer a given contract.

bottom Lowest price reached during a market cycle.

breakout A term that refers to a situation in which a commodity's price moves past a previous support or resistance level.

bull market Market in which prices are generally increasing.

buy and hold Strategy involving the purchase of commodities for the long term, typically for years at a time.

call option An exchange-traded option contract that gives the purchaser the right, but not the obligation, to enter into an underlying futures contract to buy a futures contract at a stated strike price any time prior to the option's expiration date. The grantor of the call has the obligation, on its exercise, to deliver the long futures.

carrying charges Costs incurred in warehousing the physical commodity, generally including interest, insurance, and storage.

cash settlement A finalizing mechanism in which a contract is satisfied with a cash value calculation. Cash may be given in lieu of the actual commodity, or it may be required in addition to physical delivery (for example, when commodity quality necessitates a premium or a discount). In finalizing a financial product, such as an index or foreign exchange product, cash settlement is necessary because the contract represents a value rather than a physical product.

clearinghouse An agency connected with a commodities exchange through which all futures contracts are reconciled, settled, guaranteed, and later either offset or fulfilled through delivery of the commodity and through which financial settlement is made. It may be a fully chartered separate corporation rather than a division of the exchange itself.

correction A less than 20 percent pullback in the market from its previous high.

curve fitting See *optimization*.

cyclic analysis Analysis that uses various seasonal factors as a basis for determining trends and prices.

day trade A trade that is entered into and closed out the same day.

demand An expression of the desire and ability to pay for the quantities of a commodity that potential buyers want to purchase at different prices given current conditions (e.g., prices of related goods, expectations, tastes, etc.).

dollar value (or **cash value**) The monetary value of the full amount of a commodity or financial instrument represented by a futures contract. This is the price per unit times the number of units.

downtick The situation when the sale price of a stock or commodity has fallen from its previous high.

Elliott Wave Theory A theory explaining the cyclical movements of prices by following certain indicators that predict and confirm price movements.

exercise price The predetermined price level(s), or initial "strike price," at which an underlying futures contract or an actual commodity may be established upon exercise of the option.

expiration date The last day on which an option may be exercised under the underlying futures/actual futures contract. If not exercised or assigned, the option ceases to exist.

fill-or-kill order (FOK) Also known as an immediate order, an order that must be offered or bid immediately at a given price and canceled if not executed.

foreign currency future A contract requiring the later purchase and sale of a designated amount of money issued by a foreign bank. (A March Swiss Franc contract, for example, would call for the delivery of 125,000 francs during a specified period in March.)

full carrying charge market A situation in the futures market when the price difference between delivery months reflects the full costs of interest, insurance, and storage.

fundamental analysis A process that looks at the fundamentals or basic issues of a company: price-earnings ratio (PE), future earnings potential, dividends, income, debt management, market share, and a host of other aspects. Fundamental analysis attempts to determine where a share price should be based on the company's current characteristics and future potential.

fundamentalist Someone who studies and analyzes a company's fundamentals to determine the future direction of prices

futures contract An agreement to later buy or sell a standardized amount and standardized minimum quality grade during a specific month under terms and conditions established by the federally designated contract market on which trading is conducted and at a price established in the trading pit.

futures option An option contract whose exercise results in the holder and writer of the option exchanging futures positions.

gap A term referring to the situation when the opening price of a market is higher than the previous day's high or lower than the previous day's low.

good-till-canceled order An order to buy or sell at a fixed price that remains open until executed or canceled by the customer.

hedging The initiation of a position in a futures market that is intended as a temporary substitute for the sale or purchase of the actual commodity.

initial margin Cash or securities required as a good-faith deposit to establish a specific new position in the futures or options market. An initial margin amount is set by the respective exchange. (*Note:* Initial margin is not a partial payment of the purchase.)

intermarket spread The purchase and sale of the same or different futures market on two different exchanges.

interest rate future A contract reflecting the value (and usually the later purchase or sale) of debt instruments (such as Treasury bonds or Eurodollar futures, or municipal bond futures).

intermediate-term trade A trade usually held for several months and one preferred by many traders, money managers, and investors. Intermediate-term traders seek to take advantage of larger price swings.

intramarket spread The purchase of a futures contract and sale of the same market in a different contract month or of the same or a different month, both contracts of which are trading on the same exchange.

limit order An order with some restriction(s), such as price, time, or both, on execution. Restrictions are set by the client.

limited partnership Business organization with a full flow-through of the consequences to the partners. Limited partners' liabilities are restricted, or limited, to their investment plus any debt they have agreed to be charged for. Limited partnerships must have one or more general partners whose liability is unlimited.

liquidity A term that refers to the least cost for a trader to enter and then close out a position.

local (broker) A floor broker who may trade for customers but trades primarily for her own account, continuously buying and selling for quick profits.

long-term trader A trader who may hold positions for several years, rolling contracts forward as they approach expiration. In reality, there are very few long-term futures traders.

maintenance margin The monetary value to which the original margin requirement may depreciate and still be considered a satisfactory margin to carry the established position. A minimum is specified by the governing exchange, but it may be the policy of an individual firm to set a minimum higher than that of the governing exchange's. (Note: The rule of thumb is maintenance at 75 percent of the original requirement.) The maintenance margin is also known as the *variation allowance*.

managed accounts Customer accounts for which a trading advisor or fund manager determines all trades.

margin An amount of money deposited by traders of futures contracts to ensure performance of the terms of the contract. Margin in futures is not a payment of equity or a down payment on a market itself but rather is a performance bond or security deposit.

margin call A call (usually by phone) from a clearinghouse to a clearing member, or from a brokerage firm to a customer, to bring margin deposits up to a required minimum level.

market analyst An individual who follows all important factors potentially affecting the price of the financial instrument in question. Market analysts typically distribute analyses of past market movement and forecasts of futures developments.

market entry/exit Market entry means establishing a new long, short, or spread position; market exit means closing out an existing long, short, or spread position.

market order An order to buy or sell a specified number of contracts for a specified futures contract month at the best price available at the time the order reaches the trading ring. As long as the execution price represents the best offering at the time of execution and the price received was traded approximately at the time the order entered the trading ring, any price is acceptable.

market-if-touched order (MIT) A contingency order given with a limited price instruction that becomes a market order to trade at the next best trading price when the market reaches the required price level. (Note: This type of order can be given as a sell order as well. The significant difference between an MIT order and a stop order is an MIT's location for execution relative to current prices.)

market-on-close order An instruction to buy or sell at the best price available during the closing period of the market on a given day.

market-on-the-open order An instruction to buy or sell at the best price available during the opening period of the market on a given day.

minimum fluctuation Also known as the minimum price fluctuation point or tick, the smallest increment or gradation of price movement possible in trading a given contract.

momentum A combination of volume and volatility in a commodity that keeps its price continuing in the same direction.

month abbreviations The following abbreviations are used in futures trading:

January = F	July = N
February = G	August = O
March = N	September = M
April = J	October = V
May = K	November = X
June = M	December = Z

moving average A method for averaging near-term prices in relation to long-term prices. The oldest prices are dropped as new ones are added. (Note: Moving averages are not restricted to day measurements. Any constant unit measure can be applied, and the average can be from as few as two units to whatever number of units the user wishes.)

naked option A short option position where the seller has no option or futures contract as an offset.

NQLX Hybrid exchange for trading SSFs formed by the LIFFE and Nasdaq.

offer The moment-to-moment incoming buy and sell orders received by specialists and market makers.

one-cancels-the-other-order An order designating both extremes of a trading range with different months, markets, commodities, prices, and the like. When the condition of one is reached and executed, the other is canceled.

optimization Optimizing is fitting a trading system to past data; and a trading system developer optimizes a system to generate a set of system rules that have performed well on historical data.

option writer The seller in an option trade who creates an option contract; the terms *short* and *grantor* are synonymous with *writer* and *seller*.

or-better order See *limit order*.

oscillator Type of technical analysis tool used in predicting price movements.

out trade A trade that does not match in the clearing process.

out-trade clerk An employee of a clearinghouse charged with helping to resolve problems with unmatched trade confirmations (out trades). The clearinghouse will not recognize a trade (i.e., give a trader the desired position) without confirmation of a contrary position.

pit An area of an exchange floor designed for executing orders for a given commodity.

position trader A trader who holds trades for an extended period of time. A position trader in futures is much like an investor in commodities, albeit with a shorter-time perspective, which is not necessarily limited by the life of the futures contract.

premium The additional payment allowed by exchange regulations for delivery of higher-than-required standards or grades of a commodity against a futures contract. In speaking of price relationships between different delivery months of a given commodity, one is said to be "trading at a premium" over another when its price is greater than the other. In financial instruments, a premium is the dollar amount by which a security trades above its principal value.

price order See *limit order*.

put option An exchange-traded option contract that gives the purchaser the right, but not the obligation, to enter into an underlying futures contract to be short the underlying stock or cash item at a stated strike price any time prior to the expiration of the option. The grantor of the put has the obligation, upon exercise, to deliver the short futures contract.

quote board Mechanism for displaying current prices on commodities futures contracts. The quote board is located so as to be easily seen from most positions on the trading floor.

regression Method of statistical analysis that measures quantitative correlations between different variables used to weigh hedges (hedge ratios).

relative strength indicator Technical analysis tool that attempts to indicate when the market has moved excessively in one direction and is likely to be reversed by a technical reversal.

round turn (round trip) The combination of an initiating purchase or sale of a futures contract and the offsetting sale or purchase of an equal number of futures contracts of the same delivery month.

scalper An active trader who attempts to profit on small price changes by buying and selling very short term (current trading day); a floor trader who trades only his own account and creates liquidity by buying and selling continuously.

seasonality Condition of being affected by, or occurring during, a particular period of the calendar year. This factor determines a repeatable pattern influencing supplies and prices.

short selling Generally, selling something that is not already owned. In futures, a short position not closed out requires the short seller to make delivery of the underlying asset.

short-term trader As opposed to a day trader or a position trader, one who trades for a relatively short-term market swing from two to ten days. No firm definition details the exact length of time short-term traders hold their positions.

single stock futures (SSF) A futures contract on an individual stock.

slippage The tendency for the market to fall or rise quickly, identifying buy and sell stop orders quickly. A market with too much slippage is one in which quick and sudden price moves tend to result in price fills unexpectedly or unreasonably far away from your price orders.

spot month The near month or current month in which futures trading is still possible and in which notices can be issued to the long position holder advising that delivery is about to be made. Depending on the commodity, delivery may be the physical commodity or cash settlement in lieu of the commodity.

spread The purchase of one futures contract and sale of another in the expectation that the price relationships between the two will change so that a subsequent offsetting sale and purchase will yield a net profit.

standardization The uniformity of terms and contract specifications of the futures markets to effectively interface with the cash (spot) markets enabling the economic risk and recording control (clearance).

stochastic indicator (SI) Basically, a price-derived oscillator expressed in percentages. SI values approach 0 and 100 as limits; the SI consists of two values: %K and %D. The SI period can be adjusted as desired; the shorter the period, the more the SI will fluctuate.

stock index A group of stocks selected as representative of the stock market or some industry sector. Changes in the value of the stock index are a way of measuring the changes in the stock market.

stock index futures A contract reflecting the value of a selected group of common stocks. All stock index futures are broad-based indexes reflecting movements of the overall market. These contracts can be used to hedge against, or speculate on, market moves. There is no physical delivery against any index futures; all are cash settlement contracts.

stop order See *limit order*.

strike price See *exercise price*.

supply The quantities of a futures contract or commodity that potential sellers would offer for sale at different prices given current conditions.

support The price level at which a market is expected to halt its declining trend and from which prices are expected to move higher at best, or sideways at worst.

technical analysis An analysis that utilizes charts and graphs to determine where a particular futures contract or stock price is likely to be headed in the future.

tick value The change in the dollar or cash value of a contract when a futures price changes by the minimum possible price fluctuation (one tick). The tick value is the dollar price equivalent of one tick times the number of units in the futures contract.

timing indicators/timing signals Any specific technique, whether fundamental or technical, that objectively indicates market entry, market exit, or the underlying condition (i.e., bullish, bearish, neutral) of a given market or markets. A timing indicator is also called a timing signal (the terms are used interchangeably). Timing indicators must be objective, that is, not subject to interpretation; an indicator subject to interpretation is not an indicator but rather is a technique and therefore subject to be interpreted differently by different traders and even by the same trader in different situations.

top Highest price reached during a market cycle.

trade checking The process of reconciling trade confirmations reflecting transactions that have been executed in the trading pits.

trading range Range of prices over which market action has been taking place during the time frame under study.

trading system An organized methodology (as opposed to a trading method, timing indicator, trading technique, or market pattern) containing specific market entry and exit indicators in addition to an operational set of procedures (called rules) including, but not limited to, various risk management (follow-up stop loss procedures) methods and procedures.

trading technique A fairly loose collection of procedures (as opposed to a timing indicator, timing signal, or trading system) that assists traders in making decisions about market entry or exit and is not so precise or rigid as a trading system.

trend line A line drawn across either the peaks of a price trend or price bottoms to emphasize the overall trend.

universal stock futures (USFs) Single stock futures traded at the LIFFE exchange in London.

upbid The term that refers to the condition of the bid price continuing to rise after the previous rise.

uptick The term that refers to the condition of the sales price continuing to rise after a previous rise.

volume The number of contracts that changed hands during a given period.

Index